SEMEIA 68

HONOR AND SHAME IN THE WORLD OF THE BIBLE

Guest Editors: Victor H. Matthews
Don C. Benjamin
Board Editor: Claudia Camp

©1996
by the Society of Biblical Literature

SEMEIA 68

Copyright © 1994 by the Society of Biblical Literature

All rights reserved. No part of this work may be reproduced or transmitted in any form or by any means, electronic or mechanical, including photocopying and recording, or by means of any information storage or retrieval system, except as may be expressly permitted by the 1976 Copyright Act or in writing from the publisher. Requests for permission should be addressed in writing to the Rights and Permissions Office, Society of Biblical Literature, 825 Houston Mill Road, Atlanta, GA 30329, USA.

ISSN 0095-571X
ISBN 1-58983-141-1

Printed in the United States of America
on acid-free paper

CONTENTS

Contributors to this Issue v

Introduction: Social Sciences and Biblical Studies
    Victor H. Matthews and Don C. Benjamin 7

Biblical Studies

Hebrew Bible:

1. "My Beloved Is Mine and I Am His" (Song 2:16):
The Song of Songs and Honor and Shame
    Dianne Bergant 23

2. "Return to Yahweh":
Honor and Shame in Joel
    Ronald Simkins 41

3. Honor and Shame in the David Narratives
    Gary Stansell 55

New Testament:

1. "How Honorable! How Shameful!" A Cultural Analysis
of Matthew's Makarisms and Reproaches
    K. C. Hanson 81

2. "Despising the Shame of the Cross":
Honor and Shame in the Johannine Passion Narrative
    Jerome H. Neyrey 113

Responses

1. The Anthropology of Honor and Shame:
Culture, Values, and Practice
    John K. Chance 139

2. An Anthropologist's Response to the Use
of Social Science Models in Biblical Studies
    Gideon M. Kressel 153

CONTRIBUTORS TO THIS ISSUE

Don C. Benjamin
7637 Moline St.
Houston, TX 77087
(713) 645-9035

Dianne Bergant, C.S.A.
Catholic Theological Union
5401 S. Cornell Avenue
Chicago, IL 60615
(312) 324-8000

John K. Chance
Department of Anthropology
Arizona State University
Tempe, AZ 85287-2402
(602) 965-6213

K.C. Hanson
Theology Department
Creighton University
2500 California Plaza
Omaha, NE 68178-0116
(402) 280-2507

Gideon M. Kressel
Ben Gurion University of the Negev
Beer Sheva
Israel
e-mail: kressel@bgumail.bgu.ac.il

Victor H. Matthews
Religious Studies Department
Southwest Missouri State University
Springfield, MO 65804
(417) 836-5491

Jerome H. Neyrey
Department of Theology
University of Notre Dame
Notre Dame, IN 46556
(219) 239-7469

Ronald Simkins
Theology Department
Creighton University
2500 California Plaza
Omaha, NE 68178-0116
(402) 280-2504

Gary Stansell
Religion Department
St. Olaf College
Northfield, MN 55057
(507) 646-3082

Note: The Editors thank Janet L. R. Melnyk for her work on this volume.

Social Sciences and Biblical Studies

Victor H. Matthews and Don C. Benjamin

COINCIDENCE LAUNCHED *Semeia: Honor and Shame in the World of the Bible* at the annual meeting of the Society of Bible Literature in Kansas City, MO in 1991, where we were serving as temporary program chairs for the Social Sciences and the Interpretation of Hebrew Scriptures Section. The mission of the section is to provide biblical scholars working with the social sciences a forum to report on the progress of their work, with the goal of promoting interest in the use of the social sciences in biblical interpretation, and of recruiting scholars to participate in groups which have specific commitments to study and publish on a particular area of interest. In the Social Sciences and the Interpretation of Hebrew Scriptures Section, any biblical tradition or period may be studied, and topics typically vary from paper to paper. Nonetheless, in 1991 three presenters applied social scientific studies on honor and shame to the Bible in their papers, and created the nucleus from which this volume developed.

There is no question that the social sciences have enriched the study of the Bible in recent years. The questions which prompted us to work on this volume were: "How well are biblical scholars using the social sciences in their work?" and "How could biblical scholars improve their use of the social sciences?" Therefore, we submitted five studies on honor and shame by biblical scholars to two anthropologists for review. We hope the results will provide a good introduction to honor and shame, which as a value system is a fundamental characteristic of all Mediterranean cultures, including those where ancient Israel and early Christianity took root. We also hope that the volume will make some helpful suggestions for enriching the use of the social sciences by biblical scholars in the future.

The volume first presents the works of the biblical scholars and their application of social scientific criticism to the text. Then the anthropologists Chance and Kressel will analyze how effectively the biblical scholars have used social science models and whether the categories of honor and shame apply to the texts discussed.

ABOUT THE AUTHORS:

Dianne Bergant is professor of Old Testament studies at Catholic Theological Union in Chicago. She is the general editor of *The Collegeville*

Bible Commentary (Old Testament) and was the editor of *The Bible Today* from 1986–1990. Her areas of interest include biblical interpretation, biblical spirituality, and social issues such as feminism, ecology, and peace. Her incorporation of the findings of anthropology in, "My Beloved Is Mine and I Am His (Song 2:16): Honor and Shame in the Song of Songs" is an attempt at a modified ethnographic investigation. It begins with a close reading of the Song of Songs with an eye to the character of the gender relationships depicted therein. Narrated from the woman's point of view, the Song portrays her relationship with her lover, her brothers, and the watchmen, as well as with her mother and the daughters of Jerusalem. Following the close reading, these relationships are criticized from the perspective of the categories of honor and shame.

Ronald A. Simkins teaches in the department of theology at Creighton University. His current academic interests are three-fold: myth theory and interpretation of the Bible, especially creation myths; cultural ecology of ancient Israel; and social-scientific interpretation of the Bible. "'Return to Yahweh': Honor and Shame in Joel" interprets Joel's call for the people to return (2:12–14), from the perspective of the honor/shame model. Prior scholarship has employed a covenant model with the four-fold pattern of sin-judgment-repentance-blessing in order to interpret this passage as a call to repentance. This covenant model, however, has little correspondence with the biblical text. It fails to answer the fundamental question raised by the model; "What sins of the people had brought upon them the natural catastrophe as a sign of God's judgment?" In contrast, the honor/shame model corresponds with both the vocabulary and the emphasis of the text. According to this model, Joel's call for the people to return to Yahweh is interpreted as a summons for the people to honor Yahweh by demonstrating their allegiance to him with acts of mourning appropriate to their suffering.

K.C. Hanson teaches in the department of theology at Creighton University. "How Honorable! How Shameful! A Cultural Analysis of Matthew's 'Beatitudes' and 'Woes'" observes that the formulaic character of makarisms or "beatitudes" and reproaches or "woes" has long been recognized, but argues that commentators and translators have often neglected to take these insights into account. Furthermore, their cultural and theological functions have been largely misconstrued. These forms are part of the word-field and value system of honor and shame. They exemplify the agonistic nature of Mediterranean culture. Hanson proposes the translation of "How honorable" for אַשְׁרֵי and μακάριος, and "How shameful" or "Shame on" for הוֹי and οὐαι. Linguistically these translations are confirmed by parallel terms, the antipodal character of makarisms and reproaches, as well as their literary contexts. This affects the interpretation of not only these words, but whole text-segments (Psalm 112; Luke 6:20–26). Two passages from the gospel according to Matthew (Matt 5:3–10, 23:13–36) are examined here in light of their linguistic, cultural, and theological importance. Finally the function of these two text-segments is investigated in terms of their location and function within the gospel.

Jerome H. Neyrey is professor of New Testament at the University of Notre Dame. Although he has written widely in historical criticism, his recent interests concentrate on the use of cultural anthropology and the social sciences for interpreting biblical texts, especially matters of purity and pollution, honor and shame, ritual and ceremony, economics and patronage, the social perception and control of the body, and group-oriented personality. Inasmuch as New Testament writers call the cross of Jesus a "shame," "scandal," and "foolishness," the suffering and death of Jesus are already cast in terms of honor and shame, the pivotal values of the ancients. "John 18–19: Honor and Shame and the Passion Narrative" examines the passion narrative in the Gospel according to John (John 18–19) in terms of honor and shame. First a brief synopsis is given of what honor means, how it is acquired and how it is lost, and what it looks like in terms of the physical body and its treatment. Then selected, major pericopae from the Johannine passion narrative are examined in this light, with special attention to the social dynamic of challenge and riposte, the normal way in which honor is gained or lost in ordinary social interchanges. This narrative, like others in the New Testament, embodies an ironic perspective on honor and shame, in that the ostensible shaming of Jesus is the occasion in which his honor is demonstrated, either as control of events, demonstration of power, or defense against challenge. Far from perceiving Jesus' death as shame, as his opponents would have it, the evangelist portrays Jesus both as maintaining his previous honor and even as gaining new and greater honor through his ironic enthronement as God's King.

Gary Stansell is professor of religion at St. Olaf College. He has translated several works from the German, including Wolff's commentaries on Hosea and Amos. His current research interests include honor and vengeance in the Mediterranean world and the Hebrew Bible, and the redaction and formation of the prophetic literature, especially Isaiah (Isa 28–33). "Honor and Shame in the David Narratives" examines the David Narratives in the books of Samuel in terms of the cultural values of honor and shame of the Mediterranean world. With the help of the work of cultural anthropologists, it seeks to demonstrate how honor and shame are significant in David's rise to power, in his court, family, and political life. David, at the outset of his political career a man of no honor or prestige, seeks and gains repute on his way to the position of highest honor in Israel. But the road David follows is replete with entanglements and relationships of honor and shame with Jonathan, Abigail, Michal, his children and his military forces. Many elements within the various episodes reflect the social world of the Mediterranean: the challenge-response pattern, revenge for insults, mediation between disputing parties, family solidarity, and the honor of the male bound up in the sexual purity of the female.

John K. Chance, the first of the respondents, is professor of anthropology at Arizona State University. His general interests include ethnohistory, political economy, social stratification, ethnicity, and Mesoamerica. Nearly all of his research has focused on the ethnohistory/social history of colonial Mexico. Most of his work has been done in Oaxaca, and he has written on urban Hispanic society as well as Indian peasants. He is currently involved in a long-term study of the Indian elite of a formerly Nahua, but now *mestizo*, town of central Puebla during the colonial period in the 17th and 18th centuries. The focus is on changing patterns of noble status, Indian identity, and wealth in land during that period.

Our second respondent is Gideon M. Kressel, a member of the Social Studies Unit at the J. Blaustein Institute for Desert Research, Ben Gurion University of the Negev, Israel. Much of his research has centered on land usage by Negev Bedouin and the relationships between the Bedouin and state authorities. Among his most recent publications are "Shame and Gender" (*Anthropological Quarterly* 65 [1992]: 34–46), *Descent Through Males* (Weisbaden: Harrasowitz, 1992), and "Nomadic Pastoralists, Agriculturists and the State: Self-Sufficiency and Dependence in the Middle East" (*Journal of Rural Cooperation* 21 [1993]: 33–49).

About the Topic:

The world of the Bible is now extinct, but the Bible itself remains. It was a world dramatically different from the world in which we read the Bible today. The European and North American world developed from the western Mediterranean cultures of Greece and Rome, but the world of the Bible developed in the eastern Mediterranean cultures of Mesopotamia, Syria-Palestine, Asia Minor and Egypt. There are many ways to describe the differences. The world of the Bible was eastern, virtually changeless, and agricultural. The modern western world is changing and industrial. Biblical people thought of themselves as households and their resources as limited. We think of ourselves as individuals, and our resources as renewable. Our genre of choice is history, theirs was story. In the world of the Bible there was none of the modern western separation between religion and daily life, between church and state. These differences are not accidental or superficial. They have a profound influence on how we live and how we look at life. The world view of the Bible was not right, nor is our world view wrong. These two world views are simply different from one another. Ways of thinking and doing things that were taken for granted in the world of the Bible are virtually absent from our world. Codes of honor and shame are one important example.

The biblical scholars in this volume have developed their own controlled definitions of honor and shame in the papers which follow. Nevertheless, some general remarks on honor and shame may be helpful at this point. Honor and shame are parallel labels used by anthropologists to describe either physical conditions or human behavior of which a culture approves or disapproves. In some cases, the words "honor" and "shame" actually appear in the Bible itself. But codes of honor and shame also govern the use of comparable terms like "wise" and "foolish" in the books of Proverbs, Qoheleth, and Job, as well as "clean" and "unclean" or "holiness" and "impurity" in the books of Exodus, Leviticus, and Numbers. The "Holiness Code" in the book of Leviticus (Lev 17–26), for example, is comparable to a code of honor and shame in ancient Israel.

Honor and shame are labels which defined the status of a household in the village. They do not indicate as much about what a household was actually doing or not doing, as about how villagers reacted to it. The labels are analogous to credit ratings today. They distinguished households in good social and economic standing from those that were not.

Labels teach each generation a specific way of looking at life. In the world of the Bible, some formal education on honor codes did take place in schools whose teachers explained to students why certain ways of doing things were honorable and others were shameful. But most education was informal, and labelling was the principal means of informal education. Villagers applied labels with words, gestures, facial expressions, or tone of voice.

Honor entitled a household to life. Honorable households ate moderately, did not get drunk, worked hard, made good friends, sought advice before acting, held their temper, paid their taxes, and imposed fair legal judgments. They were careful in dealing with one another during menstruation, sexual intercourse, childbirth, and death. And they were equally conscientious about what food they ate, what clothes they wore, what animals they herded and what crops they planted in their fields. Honorable households could care for their own members and were prepared to help their neighbors. They were households in good standing, licensed to make a living in the village and entitled to its support. Only honorable households were entitled to buy, sell, trade, marry, arrange marriages, serve in assemblies, and send warriors to the tribe. Only honorable households were entitled to make wills, appoint heirs, and serve as legal guardians to care for households endangered by drought, war, and epidemic. Honorable households were in place and functioning well.

Shame sentenced a household to death by placing its land and children in jeopardy. Shamed households ate too much, drank too much, were lazy, quarrelsome, selfish, and thought nothing about lying to the village assembly. They were thoughtless in their sexual relationships, and disrespectful of the new born and the dead. Their herds were mangy, and their farms run down. Shamed households did not fulfill their responsibilities to their own members or their neighbors. Shamed households were on probation. They were out-of-place and not functioning properly. Consequently, both their contributions to the village and their eligibility for its support were suspended. The label downgraded the status of a household, until it demonstrated that it was once again contributing to the village.

Despite all the differences between the world in which the Bible developed and the world in which we use the Bible today, there is still a common humanity and a common search for a fully human life which draws these two worlds together. In both worlds there are people searching for their proper place with one another, with nature and with their God. Anthropology can help explain many of the relationships between today's world in which the Bible is read and that in which the Bible developed.

Anthropology, like sociology, economics, political science, and psychology, is a social science. It is the study of human life and human culture, and particularly life and culture outside Europe and North America. Anthropologists gather data by observation, not by laboratory experiment. Among other things, they use this data to determine what kind of creatures in pre-history are to be classified as human, how humans were distributed over the earth, how humans organize, how human social institutions, arts, and sciences develop, and the extent to which necessity, reason, and luck influence physical and cultural development.

Anthropologists continue to refine and expand the basic principles that they use. They assume that the physical ability of humans influences the cultures which they develop. The reverse is also assumed. Physical and cultural anthropology are interdependent. Many important human physical developments were stimulated by cultural evolution. The cultural development of hunting, for example, is believed to have encouraged upright posture, fine motor skills needed to make weapons, and the expansion of the brain in order to hunt more intelligently. Nature influences nurture, and nurture influences nature.

Anthropologists also assume that the relationship between humans and their natural environment is comparable to the relationship between nature and nurture (Simkins 1994:15–41). Nature influences the physical and the cultural development of humans, and humans impact the development of nature.

Anthropologists today do not assume social evolution or progress, although such assumptions were once common. Herbert Spencer (1820–1903) is best known as a proponent of social evolution. For Spencer, all cultures begin as small homogeneous bands, which increase in size and create competition for goods and services, requiring more complex social organization. This model of social change and the assumption that all things inevitably evolve from the simple to the complex influenced many reconstructions of the world of the Bible. Today, it is clearer that cultures can appear at any level of complexity without passing through a fixed process from simple to complex. And when cultures do develop, they can move from complex to simple as often as from simple to complex. For example, Norman K. Gottwald (1979) has argued that early Israel (1250–1000 BCE) was a "retribalization movement" from the more complex culture of the Late Bronze period (1500–1250 BCE) to a simpler and more decentralized village culture.

Early cross-cultural studies were often also flawed by anachronism, which assumed that all cultures functioned in the same way. Anachronism is the projection of the patterns and dynamics of life in one culture onto another. The world of the Bible has been repeatedly reconstructed as if it were a European or an industrial world driven by capitalism and individualism. All too often the world of the Bible and the values and behavior of its people were portrayed as if they were modern Americans or Europeans. Today, anthropologists are careful to find useful, valid ways of discovering how people in another culture think and act.

Anthropologists strive not to assess the social institutions in cultures they study in relationship to their own cultures, although such ethnocentricism is difficult to avoid. Cultures which differ from European or American cultures are not, because of that difference alone, labeled "primitive" or "savage." Several developments after 1900 led to the denunciation of ethnocentrism. The brutality of colonization in Asia, Africa, and the Americas ultimately raised questions about the superiority of European culture over those it dominated and destroyed. The science on which European culture was founded now seemed to be creating as much suffering as it alleviated. Fieldwork by European anthropologists among so-called "primitive" or "savage" peoples began to create more understanding of and respect for their ways of life as not only different from, but in some ways superior to, those in Europe (Eilberg-Schwartz 1990:2).

Although the academic discipline of anthropology is modern, anthropological interests are ancient and on-going. There was an interest in the world of the Bible even before it was canonized in the shape we have it today. Ancient geographers, for example, noted that the Mount of Olives ". . . lies before Jerusalem on the east" (Zech 14:14), and ancient ethnographers explained that ". . . the one who is now called a prophet was formerly called a seer" (1 Sam 9:9).

Herodotus (484–425 BCE) has often been called the first anthropologist. More than half of the nine volumes in his *History* study the peoples known to the Greeks under the same basic categories used in anthropology today. He describes the kinship, marriage, economics, technology, and religion of the peoples whom he encounters. Nonetheless, Herodotus was fiercely ethnocentric. He judged every other culture on the basis of Greek culture, and thus concluded that all other cultures were barbaric.

During the renaissance, a concern for the world of the Bible also appears in the interpretive tradition. Cornelius Bertramus published a book on the relationship of religion and government in ancient Israel (1574), Cavolus Sigonius a study of biblical politics (1583), and Martinus Geier a work on biblical ritual (1656). Johannes Henricus Ursinus concentrated his research on the trees of the Bible (1663), and Hadrianus Relandus wrote a book on the monuments of antiquity in Palestine (1716).

Attitudes of Europeans toward non-Europeans took time to develop from simple curiosity to academic anthropology. The trajectory began in periods of ignorance when Europeans were simply unaware that there were any other cultures but their own. While building their empires, Europeans inevitably developed on-going relationships with native peoples in Asia, Africa and, America. Anthropologists studied these peoples as Europeans attempted to understand these very different cultures. Similarities between their cultures and the world of the Bible were provocative, but went unexplored, to some extent because of the threat which these similarities posed to the status of Judaism and Christianity. Were Judaism and Christianity unique, divinely-revealed religions, or simply human cultures of the ancient Near East like those of Africa and America? Were Judaism and Christianity superior to, or simply comparable to the human cultures of Asia, Africa, and America?

Scholars of the day assumed that, even if Judaism and Christianity were not unique and divinely-revealed religions, they were, at least, superior to the cultures of Asia, Africa, and America. Consequently, scholars devoted their energy toward explaining away the similarities instead of learning something about the world of the Bible from them. For some, the similarities between the cultures or Asia, Africa, and America and the world of the Bible were either non-existent or superficial. For others, these similarities were real, but they were accidental rather than essential. Another tradition of interpretation viewed the similarities as the result of corruption from "pagan" cultures. Finally, there were those who felt that the similarities reflected primitive practices beyond which the world of the Bible eventually evolved (Eilberg-Schwartz 1990:49–66).

Europeans alternated between downgrading the cultures of Asia, Africa, and America and idealizing them. Christians of the Dark Ages in Europe (476–1000 CE) considered life a mystery which only revelation could interpret. They considered non-Christian traditions and rituals to be superstition and magic, whose success in interpreting life was inconsistent and coincidental. In contrast, Enlightenment Rationalists (1700–1800 CE) considered life to be a single great mental puzzle or syllogism, not a mystery. For them, the human mind could interpret human life quite adequately without revelation. Rationalists considered the peoples of Asia, Africa, and America to be savages who thought little or not at all. For them, savages were virtually identical to the earliest humans, and inferior to more evolved Christians. Savage traditions and rituals were primitive forms of human logic. For the Romantics (1800–1900 CE), life was rich and diverse, and not a unity. It was better interpreted by feelings, and without logic. For them, the peoples of Asia, Africa, and America, who thought little or not at all, were noble. Unlike Europeans whose logic corrupted their society and polluted their environment, they lived emotionally and spontaneously and were models for reforming European society (see Eilberg-Schwartz: 41–86).

Both the "brutal savage" and the "noble savage" theories have been more recently recognized as ethnocentric or racist. Anthropologists who consider their own race superior distort their theories and fieldwork as badly as those who consider the races they study superior. Europe cannot be used to evaluate Asia, Africa, and America, and Asia, Africa, and America cannot be used to evaluate Europe, as long as one is considered superior to the other. The brutal savage theory denigrated every culture but Europe. The noble savage theory idealized every culture but Europe, and eliminated words like "savage," "primitive," "barbaric" and "pagan" from the technical vocabulary of anthropology. Both assumed that the culture of Europe was completely logical, and the cultures of Asia, Africa, and America were completely emotional. Eventually it became apparent that all cultures develop from both logic and feelings, and that the cultures of Asia, Africa, and America possessed sophisticated forms of logic. Both the brutal and noble savage theories use the relationship between Christians and Jews in Europe as a model for the relationship between European culture and the cultures of Asia, Africa, and America. Neither studied Asia, Africa, and America on their own merits, which would show that all cultures enjoy relative success and failure in dealing with their natural environments and developing a functional society. No culture is completely noble, or completely savage. For example, some aspects of cultures in Asia, Africa, and America are environmentally sensitive, others are as destructive and wasteful as the factories of Europe's industrial revolution (Eilberg-Schwartz 1990:31–48).

Anthropologists today are reappraising their definitions of culture. Standard definitions emphasized the differences between cultures and viewed culture as a way of life shared by all inhabitants of a region. The real world, both ancient and modern, is far less clear and distinct. People living together often do not share a uniform culture. And cultures often do not respect geographic boundaries. Cultures in one part of the world interact with cultures in another. The world is far more interconnected than past definitions admitted. Therefore, anthropologists are now redefining their field in this transcultural world that does not divide itself clearly at the joints into societies or traditions, a fact which makes the analysis of culture a far more awkward enterprise. Migration, technology, and market forces have created more interaction among cultures than anthropologists, to date, have adequately studied.

Another significant change taking place in anthropology today is the realization that anthropologists cannot simply record human differences. They need to look seriously at the dynamic of human interactions. The lack of study of human interactions and the emphasis on cultural differences has contributed to cultural conflicts varying in severity from the culture wars which pit a curriculum based on Western civilization against multiculturalism to such tragedies as ethnic cleansing. To argue that all cultures must be judged by their own standards has too often forced scholars to suspend ethical judgment. Anthropologists are beginning to abandon their cultural relativism and become witnesses who not only record, but also react to events. They are becoming more and more willing to name the wrongs that they see and to hold themselves accountable when they fail to notice key ethical dilemmas.

During the nineteenth century W. Robertson Smith (1846–1894) was among the first to introduce anthropology into his study of the Bible by comparing the culture of ancient Israel with the culture of Bedouin Arabs. Similar studies were done by Adolphe Lods (1867–1948) and Antonin Causse (1877–1948).

But it was during the twentieth century that the ground-breaking work of Hermann Gunkel on biblical folklore (1917), of Sigmund Mowinckel (1884–1966) on storytelling (1921–24), of Alfred Bertholet (1919), Johannes Pedersen (1920), and of Gustaf Dalman (1928–39) on the culture of biblical Israel, pioneered the use of anthropology in biblical interpretation. Slowly it became apparent that while naming and dating the principal persons, places, and events may be appropriate for understanding written literature, oral tradition has an anonymity that avoids names and a timelessness that blurs dates. Interpreting oral tradition requires an understanding of the social institutions (German: *Sitz im Leben*) where these traditions developed and were told. Social institutions use oral traditions to educate and to motivate people in the essentials of survival. It is as important to study Israel's social institutions in order to understand its traditions as it is to study Israel's traditions in order to understand its social institutions.

Despite these breakthroughs, few biblical scholars immediately began using anthropology. There was the work of Albrecht Alt on the early forms of Israelite tradition and state development (1925, 1929, 1930), of Roland de Vaux, who attempted a reconstruction of the life and institutions of ancient Israel (1958), and of Martin Noth, who examined Israel's tribal system (1960). While anthropology proved invaluable for understanding traditional cultures encountered by empire-building nations, yet for theological reasons it was not widely used to understand the equally traditional cultures of the Bible. The delay was due, in part, to the widespread understanding that biblical religions were higher or revealed religions. Anthropology could study lower religions which evolved from human experience, but there was nothing human or savage in Judaism and Christianity for anthropology to study.

In the 20th century, debates between students of text and tell further delayed the development of an anthropology of the Bible. It took time to realize that anthropology is no less text-based than biblical or ancient Near Eastern studies. One relies on the ethnographies composed by skilled modern observers, the other on texts from the ancient world. Neither is an objective data base. Insiders are not necessarily better interpreters of culture than outsiders, nor modern ethnographies better interpretations than ancient texts (Geertz 1973). It became essential for both anthropologists and biblical scholars to weigh the credentials of their informants carefully. The work of the scholar of ancient Israel uses biblical texts to study the culture, whereas the anthropologist must study the ethnographies of other anthropologists to study a culture. In essence both disciplines rely on a text for social interpretation. However, in biblical studies it is the people whose culture is the object of the study who create the text, whereas in anthropology it is the anthropologist who creates the text which the anthropologist then studies.

Although some biblical scholars were willing to compare and contrast Israel with contemporaneous ancient Near Eastern cultures, they were unwilling to draw on anthropological studies outside the world of the Bible itself. Yet, there is no inherent reason that metonymic or synchronic studies of cultures related in time and geography to ancient Israel are more valid or helpful to understanding the world of the Bible than metaphoric or diachronic studies of cultures separated in geography and time from ancient Israel.

Some early cross-cultural studies degenerated into what has been called "parallelomania." This abuse of parallelism almost caused biblical scholars to discard, rather than refine, cross-cultural studies. Slowly, they became aware of how difficult it is to find truly comparable elements. This resulted in a concern to study social institutions in context, and to create the interpretive context carefully. Because literary and material remains produce an incomplete picture of a culture, it is essential to reconstruct from these fragments something of the whole. The archaeology of culture involves interpreters in the attempt to imagine how incomplete literary and material remains may reflect or distort a culture of which they once formed only a part. Anthropologists and biblical scholars are both engaged in an archaeology of culture.

Early cross-cultural studies also made biblical scholars aware that cultures may employ the same ideas and yet differ profoundly from one another in their essential nature. Therefore, they began to restrict their comparisons to those phenomena which have been proved to be effects of the same causes.

Despite the slowed interests of biblical scholars in anthropology, the interest of anthropologists in the world of the Bible continued (Lewis 1981; Kapelrud 1967; Eliade 1964; Evans-Pritchard 1964). If, as Marx maintained, the forces which bring about cultural change are not ideological but social and economic, then the social sciences can be used to understand why important cultural changes took place. In opposition to this dialectical materialism, Max Weber held that new ideas or values change cultures. To demonstrate this thesis, Weber made the first sociological study of ancient Israel: *Ancient Judaism* (1920).

Another classical study of the period was *Myth, Legend and Custom in the Old Testament* by Theodor Gaster, who pursued Gunkel's interests in folklore (1950, 1969). Gaster also stands in the tradition of Edward B. Tylor (1832–1917) and James G. Frazer (1854–1941). Tylor developed a thesis called the "doctrine of survivals," which argued that beliefs often survive the end of the simple cultures in which they develop and are adopted by more and more complex cultures. Simple cultures, for Tylor, develop animistic beliefs, which eventually evolve into polytheism and then into monotheism in the more complex cultures which adopt them. In *The Golden Bough*, Frazer created an archive of beliefs which he traced, using Tylor's thesis, from magic to monotheism. Gaster applied Frazer's work and method to the Old Testament.

By the end of the 20th century, the long overdue anthropology of the Bible began to take shape, and students discovered how fascinating and truly human the previously ignored world of the Bible can be. Biblical scholars were applying the work of anthropologists to virtually every area of daily life in the world of the Bible. Some of the most important work being done by anthropologists today is being applied to the Bible and its world, as the bibliography for this volume certainly testifies.

Culture is a always a delicate blend of story and daily living, of mythos and ethos. Mythos is the story a people tell, ethos is the way a people live. Biblical scholars study one; anthropologists the other. It is impossible to understand any culture, ancient or modern, without studying both. Stories make sense only in the light of the social institutions that shape them and social institutions are intelligible only when they are interpreted in stories. Biblical people preserved their cultural identity not simply by repeating their stories, but by developing social institutions which reflected their values. To divorce mythos and ethos, to study only the Bible without its social world, incorrectly assumes that ideas alone, disconnected from material and social reality, have the power to transform individuals and society. They do not. If we are to continue to study the Bible profitably, we must better understand the world from which it comes. Certainly the contributors to *Semeia: Honor and Shame in the World of the Bible* have dedicated themselves generously to this task.

WORKS CITED

Alt, A.
    1925   "Die Landnahme der Israeliten in Palastina." *Reformationsprogramm der Universitat.* Leipzig.
    1929   "Der Gott der Vater." *Beitrage zur Wissenschaft vom Alten und Neuen Testament.* Stuttgart.
    1930   "Die Staatenbildung der Israeliten in Palastina." *Reformationsprogramm der Universitat.* Leipzig.

Bertramus, C.
    1574   *De politica Judaica tam civili quam ecclesiastica.*

Bertholet, A.
    1919   *Kulturgeschichte Israels.* Berlin.

Dalman, G.
    1928   *Arbeit und Sitte in Palastina.* Gutersloh: C. Bertelsmann.

Eilberg-Schwartz, H.
    1990   *The Savage in Judaism: An Anthropology of Israelite Religion and Ancient Judaism*. Bloomington: Indiana University Press.

Eliade, M.
    1964   *Shamanism: Archaic Techniques of Ecstasy*. New York: Pantheon.

Evans-Pritchard, E.E.
    1964   *Social Anthropology and Other Essays*. New York: Free Press.

Gaster, T.H.
    1950   *Thespis: Ritual, Myth and Drama in the Ancient Near East*. New York: Schuman.
    1969   *Myth, Legend and Custom in the Old Testament*. New York: Harper & Row.

Geertz, C.
    1973   *The Interpretation of Cultures: Selected Essays*. New York: Basic Books.

Geier, M.
    1656   *De Ebraeorum luctu lugentiumque ritibus*.

Gottwald, N.K.
    1979   *The Tribes of Yahweh. A Sociology of the Religion of Liberated Israel 1250–1050 B.C.E.*. New York: Orbis.

Gunkel, H.
    1917   *Das Marchen im Alten Testament*. Tübingen.

Kapelrud, A.S.
    1967   "Shamanistic Features in the Old Testament." Pp. 90–96 in *Studies in Shamanism*. Ed. Carl-Martin Edsman. Stockholm: Almqvist and Wiksell.

Mowinckel, S.
    1962   *The Psalms in Israel's Worship*, 2 vols. [originally published as Psalmenstudien I-IV (1921–1924)]. Oxford: Blackwell.

Lewis, I.M.
    1971   *Ecstatic Religion: An Anthropological Study of Spirit Possession and Shamanism*. Baltimore: Penguin.

Noth, M.
    1960   *The History of Israel*. Trans. P.R. Ackroyd. 2nd edition. New York: Harper & Row.

Pedersen, J.
    1920   *Israel, Its Life and Culture*. London: Oxford University Press.

Relandus, H.
    1716   *Palaestina ex monumentis veteribus illustrata*.

Sigonius, C.
    1583   *De re publica Hebraeorum libri septem*.

Simkins, R.A.
    1994   *Creator and Creation*. Peabody, MA: Hendrickson.

Ursinus, J.H.
   1663   *Arboretum Biblicum.*

de Vaux, R.
   1958   *Ancient Israel.* New York: McGraw-Hill.

Weber, M.
   1920   *Ancient Judaism.* Trans. and ed. Hans H. Gerth and Don Martindale. Glencoe: Free Press [1952].

"MY BELOVED IS MINE AND I AM HIS" (SONG 2:16): THE SONG OF SONGS AND HONOR AND SHAME

Dianne Bergant
Catholic Theological Union

ABSTRACT

The incorporation of the findings of anthropology into biblical studies has opened a significant new avenue for critical biblical interpretation. While most of the work done in this area has been primarily ethnological, the present article is an attempt at a modified ethnographic investigation. It begins with a close reading of the Song of Songs, with an eye to the character of the gender relationships depicted therein. Narrated from the woman's point of view, the Song portrays her relationship with her lover, her brothers, and the watchmen, as well as with her mother and the daughters of Jerusalem. Following this close reading, the relationships are critiqued from the perspective of the categories of honor and shame.

THE TASK AND THE METHOD

Biblical studies have witnessed a growing interest in the application of the findings of the human sciences to the investigation of Scripture. This is especially true of the field of anthropology. Formerly called "comparative sociology,"[1] anthropology is specifically interested in the way meaning both varies and converges across cultures. Over the years anthropology itself developed in several different directions. The primary object of cultural anthropology, the type normally pursued in North America, is "culture" as it illuminates and helps to interpret human behavior. The tradition of cultural anthropology goes back to Boas (1955) and Kroeber (1952) and can trace its development through the functionalist theories of culture developed by Malinowski. British anthropology, on the other hand, developed rather differently. From Malinowski

---

[1] The British anthropologist A.R. Radcliffe-Brown (1881–1955), who coined the phrase "comparative sociology," stands with Bronislaw Malinowski as founder of modern anthropology. Malinowski attempted to explain the function of social institutions by reference to biological needs, while the more theoretical Radcliffe-Brown turned to the French *Année Sociologique* school of Durkheim and Mauss. Malinowski's biological model focused on *cultural* forces; Radcliffe-Brown's sociological theorizing led him to explanations in terms of *social* forces: society, not individual organisms or cultural artifacts, is the proper subject/object of study (cf. Lewis:55f).

through Radcliffe-Brown's structural-functionalism, it focused more clearly on social relations, seeing "society," in a Durkheimian sense (Durkheim 1961), rather than "culture" as the focus of study. Evans-Pritchard brilliantly rooted ethnographic analysis in a study of social organization, moving away from the rather deterministic and static functionalism of his predecessors to a more dynamic structuralism.

The anthropological approach of this article is in the tradition of social anthropology, which constitutes a somewhat different approach to biblical interpretation than does one derived from a cultural anthropology perspective (e.g. Malina; Malina and Neyrey). Social anthropology, which is concerned with social relations, seeks an understanding of meaning-in-context, as well as linkage between the things, people, and relationships it studies on the one hand and the person and the world of the one who undertakes the study (Worgul: 5; Geertz 1988; Jackson; Okely and Callaway). The method employed in this article has more in common with ethnography, descriptive accounting of human societies, than with ethnology, classification according to cultural characteristics (Beattie: 16–22). In its attempt to use methods from the field of social anthropology, it perceives the fictive world of the biblical text as an admittedly limited yet authentic ancient socio-cultural setting within which the social dynamics of the agents can be observed. Such an approach has already been suggested by Edmund Leach, a prominent social anthropologist (1976:85). He proposes this, because he maintains that "the Bible has the characteristics of mythohistory of the sort which anthropologists regularly encounter when they engage in present-day field research" (1983:21).

Though in practice the approaches of ethnography and ethnology may often converge, theoretically at least they are distinguishable. Ethnography seeks to gather empirical data; ethnology catalogs ethnographic findings. If an ethnographer inscribes social discourse by writing it down (Geertz 1973:19), then, presumably, one should be able to recover some degree of this social discourse by analyzing the inscription. The approach employed in this study attempts to produce what anthropologists call a "thick description" of behavior (Geertz 1973:3–30). This is a highly detailed analysis which explicitly includes, as far as is possible, the insider's perspective (the emic, cf. Harris). A "thick description" is achieved through a process of radical empiricism known as "participant observation" (Jorgensen; Jackson). Concerned with empirical data, it begins with a particular life situation (the dynamics within the Song of Songs) and moves toward a contextualized understanding of meaning. The findings of historical research enter the investigation as little as possible at this point. Only after the data is examined within its own context is it tested against ethnological findings. Conclusions are drawn by induction as well as by comparison.

Introduction to the Book

"All the world is not worth the day that the Song of Songs was given to Israel; all the *Kĕtûbîm* are holy but the Song of Songs is the holy of holies" (Mishna Yadaim, 3:5). Two notable studies of the Song of Songs (Exum: 47; Gordis: 1) begin with this rabbinic quote, which both represents the reverence in which its advocates have held the book and, for the sake of its skeptics, justifies its inclusion in the canon. The book itself has generated considerable controversy regarding its literary integrity, its genre, its structure, and its interpretation. Some scholars contend that the book is really an anthology of discrete poems (Landsberger 1954). Today, most believe that the eight chapters should be interpreted as a unit, albeit one that is composed of several different poems. Neither opinion adequately addresses all of the questions about the book's composition, yet some view must be espoused if one is to engage in critical analysis of it. Since the fictive world of the text is here regarded as a socio-cultural setting, this study presumes some form of literary unity.

Although there is general agreement about the erotic nature of this lyric poetry, this is not the case regarding the overall literary character of the book. There are basically four ways that the Song has been interpreted: allegorically (Robert), as a cultic reenactment (Pope), as a dramatic performance (Pouget & Guitton) and literally (Murphy). Each of these interpretive approaches reveals different facets of the literary quality of the book and opens up possibilities for understanding the social dynamics depicted there. The book does in fact contain certain features that lend themselves to one or other of these approaches. For example, the marriage metaphor used to characterize the love relationship between first YHWH and Israel (Isa 54:5; Hos 2:14-20) and later Christ and the Church (2 Cor 11:2; Rev 19:6b-8) provides a precedent for allegorical interpretation of the social dynamics. Parallels with the vocabulary and themes of ancient fertility rituals persuade others to look for literary origins in the sacred marriages rites of Damuzi/Inanna (Tammuz/Ishtar). The patterns of such rites will influence the way the interaction is understood. Still others see the basic features of a drama in the absence of a narrator and the inclusion of refrains and choruses. Finally, the similarity between these poems and some Egyptian love poems has led many to conclude that the Song of Songs is made up of lyric love poems, some of which recount the physical charms of the loved one (similar to the Arabic *wasf*) while others describe erotic longing.

The ambiguity in interpretation has led some to maintain that any supposed structure is brought to the book by the interpreter rather than found within the text itself. It is interesting to note that while the first and preferred method of interpretation of most of the Bible traditionally has been the literal approach, the opposite has been true with this book. It seems that much of the sexual imagery has been either so explicit or so suggestive as to offend the sensitivities of many of the faithful. This and the fact that there is no mention of God in the entire book have brought some to believe that originally the poems were secular. Until recently, however, most commentators presumed that the poems were not to be understood literally but must have some concealed religious meaning. (A comprehensive treatment of the history of the Song's interpretation is found in Pope: 89–229.)

There is even more variance in determining the structure of the book. Different deciding criteria have yielded various designs and numbering of the poems. The total number has ranged from twelve to fifty-two; the median being about thirty (Elliot: 20). While the composition of the book is not the principal concern of this study, a decision regarding its literary structure is the first step in any serious analysis. The boundaries of the fictive world must be established before analysis of any of its social dynamics can commence. The present critical reading will be facilitated by the following division: 1:1; 1:2–2:7; 2:8–3:5; 3:6–5:1; 5:2–6:3; 6:4–8:4; 8:5–14. 1:1 is an obvious superscription. Verses 5:2–6:3 form probably the most clearly defined poetic unit (Exum: 50–53; Gordis: 36f; 88–92; Fox: 139–149; Elliot: 122–148; Murphy 1990:164–175). The passage in 2:8–3:5 has also been recognized as a distinct unit (Elliot: 67–82; Exum isolates the unit but maintains that it begins with the refrain in 2:7 [53–56]; Murphy concurs with Exum's basic division, but disputes beginning the unit with 2:7, [1990:63]). Verses 1:2–2:7 and 8:5–14 comprise distinct units (contra Exum, 1:2–2:6 and 8:4–14) as do 3:6–5:1 and 6:4–8:4 (Exum: 61–74; Elliot: 43–66, 83–121, 149–214; Murphy 1990:190–200).

The superscription (1:1) performs several significant functions. It identifies the book's genre as a song, the singular form of "song" indicates the literary unity of its final form, and it accords both authoritative and religious Solomonic legitimation to the work. The Hebrew construction of שִׁיר הַשִּׁירִים ("Song of Songs") suggests that the phrase is less the title of the book than a superlative construct intended to set this song apart from all other songs. The significance of these matters should not be underestimated. Their import will be clear when the implications of the present investigation are considered.

The first unit (1:2–2:7) consists of a lyric speech of the woman (vv.2–7) and a series of poems wherein the woman and man proclaim their mutual admiration (1:8–2:7). The shift between second and third person (1:2), a poetic device known as enallage, is less confusing than is any attempt at determining with certainty the identity of the voice at each point in the unit (e.g., who is speaking in 1:8, the man or the daughters?). The closing refrain (2:6f) includes a solemn adjuration directed to the daughters of Jerusalem. The second unit (2:8–3:5) ends with the identical adjuration (3:5). Here the woman's lyric includes a poetic reminiscence of an encounter with the man (2:10–14). The third unit (3:6–5:1) begins with a segment that is clearly independent but difficult to ascribe with certainty to a particular voice (3:6–11). This is followed by a tribute to the beauty of her body (4:1–7) and an admiration poem (4:8–5:1), both attributed to the man. The fourth unit (5:2–6:3) consists of both narrative and dialogue. The woman recounts an encounter with the man (5:2–7), and then praises the charms of the man's body (5:10–16) and garden imagery (6:2–3). The fifth unit (6:4–8:4) consists of several different genres ascribed to the male voice (6:4–7:10a[9a], and an amorous reply of the woman which closes with an adjuration (7:10b[9b]-8:4). If any part of the Song can be called a collection of disparate poems, it is the final unit (8:5–14). Neither is there continuity from one part to the next, nor is the specific voice always identifiable. The high point of the Song is found here in vv. 6–7. The book itself ends on such a strange note that some believe the real ending has been lost.

Finally, form critical study has provided genre classification which can assist in understanding this rather complex literary creation. The material can be identified as: poems of yearning (1:2–4; 2:6; 7:9b-10[8b-9]; 8:1–3); self-descriptions (1:5–6; 8:10), poems of admiration (1:9–17; 2:3; 4:9–15; 6:4–5a; 7:8); accounts of an experience (2:8–10a; 3:1–5; 5:2–8; 6:11–12; 8:5b); characterizations of the physical charms of the loved one (4:1–7; 5:10–16; 6:5b-7; 7:2–8[1–7]); invitations to tryst (2:10b-14; 4:8; 5:1; 7:12–14[11–13]). (For different classifications see Gordis: 35f; Murphy, 1981:101–103; Fox: 271–7.) Genre identification and some understanding of the rhetorical function of a particular genre are crucial if the "participant observer" is to grasp the sense of the dialogue.

The Song of Songs is unique in that it is the only book of the Bible to have all of its content in the form of speeches; there is no straightforward narration. This direct speech, a feature which provides a better insight into the disposition of the speaker than does mere narrative reporting (Alter), opens the book to analysis through an examination of the characterization revealed through the lyrics (cf. Fox: 253–66). The major speakers are the woman and the man. In addition to the lovers, other gender-specific groups can be distinguished, the daughters of Jerusalem, the watchmen, and the woman's brothers. A delineation of these characterizations, derived from a kind of "participant observation," should provide some insight into the gender relationships portrayed in the book. These relationships will then be analyzed from the perspective of the anthropological categories of honor and shame (Peristiany; Malina; Gilmore) in order to see if and how these categories can throw light on an understanding of the text.

The Shulammite

A close reading of the Song of Songs reveals a remarkable woman identified as the Shulammite, perhaps the feminine form of the name Solomon (7:1[6:13]). Some translations refer to her as a girl or a maiden, in order further to portray her presumed unmarried state. However, the connotation of youthfulness carried by these nouns also suggests immaturity, a trait that conflicts with the book's depiction of the woman. Refuting her brothers' impression of her (8:8), she describes herself as full-figured (8:10). Furthermore, she is quite independent of societal restraints, in contrast to women in a patriarchal society. While she may be rather young, this is a mature woman, not an naive girl.

Although the Song is a tribute to mutual love, the principal frame of reference is the amorous disposition of the woman. Her words open and close the Song and her voice is dominant throughout (cf. Trible: 144–65). Most of the poems of yearning are uttered by her (1:2–4; 2:6; 8:1–3. 7:9b–10[10b–11] is an exchange between the lovers). She is the one who is portrayed as lovesick (2:5; 5:8), and longing to follow her beloved should he bid her come with him (1:4), and it is she who celebrates their mutual belonging (2:16–17; 6:3). She takes the initiative, seeking him both in the privacy of her room (3:1; 5:6b) and in public streets of the city (3:2; 5:7). Her concern to protect their love from public scrutiny and the possibility of criticism (1:7; 8:1) does not prevent her from venturing out, alone at night, in search of him, even jeopardizing her own safety. She is neither slow to speak erotically about their union (1:2,4,13; 3:4) nor embarrassed by the titillating language that he uses to describe her body (4:5–6; 7:2–10a[1–9a]). It is clear that the woman depicted in the Song is driven by love, not inhibited by social opinion or by some narrow sense of sexual propriety.

The family relationships of the woman are also of note. Nowhere in the book is there a reference to her father. Her brothers seem to have assumed responsibility for her (1:6; 8:8), a practice quite common in patriarchal societies. However, she does not appear to agree with their perception of her degree of maturity nor with the overbearing nature of their attempts at supervision. In fact, her behavior indicates that she disregards any restraint placed on her by them. If there is a prominent family member, it is her mother. Her siblings are not even called brothers. Rather, their identification is through their maternal relationship; they are her mother's sons (1:6; 8:1). The Shulammite herself is acclaimed "the darling of her mother" (6:9). One of the places where she would tryst with her lover is her mother's house (3:4; 8:2). One might say that this is not unusual, since women's concerns and activity are often restricted to women's worlds and quarters. However, rendezvous in vineyards and excursions into city streets and squares, hardly private and secluded places, suggest access to a broader world. Careful observation reveals a significant degree of female prominence and independence.

The Shulammite's description of the charms of her lover and the pleasures of their lovemaking, though often symbolic, is quite provocative. Her beloved is comely and agile like a young stag—an animal renowned for its sexual prowess (2:8–9,17; 8:14). The beauty of his body is extolled part by part from his head to his thighs (5:10–15 [a *wasf*, cf. Falk: 125–35]). She rhapsodizes about the impassioned delights they experience that intoxicate like wine (1:2; 2:4; 7:10) and about those that can be savored as one savors luscious fruits (2:3; 4:16; 7:14). She relates how various luxurious aromas enhance the ardor of their passion (1:3,12–14; 6:2). Sensuous metaphors such as these not only evoke vivid images but can arouse desire as well. This woman is not intimidated by eroticism.

The words of the young man are either in answer to the woman's questions or in dialogue with her. They provide the reader with a glimpse of the woman as perceived by her companion in love. His first words acclaim her as beautiful (1:15; also 2:10b,13; 4:1,7; 6:4,10; 7:7), the fairest among women (1:8; also 5:9; 6:1). No other woman can compare with her (2:2; 6:8–10); her beauty is unblemished (4:7). The jewelry that adorns her makes her resplendence rival the most ornate of Pharaoh's chariots (1:9–11). Her eyes have enraptured him (4:9; 6:5), even though they are as gentle and innocent as doves (1:15; 4:1). Every part of her body is comely (4:1–5; 6:5b–7; 7:2–6; also (7:8–10a), and her voice is sweet to the ear (2:14). He compares her to a garden that is fruitful yet inaccessible to all but him (4:12–15; 5:1). This is a man who has been smitten by love. His interest in the woman is certainly erotic, but there is no indication that he desires her merely for his own pleasure. The desire described in these poems is mutual, seeking mutual fulfillment. The woman is not being used; she is being loved.

The character of the other people mentioned in the Song also points out the prominence of the Shulammite. They are directly involved only with her and not with the man. The daughters of Jerusalem act as a kind of foil for the woman. Since there are no soliloquies in the Song, she is most likely addressing them when it is clear that she is not speaking to the man (Fox: 253–66). They pose questions (3:6; 5:9; 6:1) to which she provides answers, thus facilitating the forward movement of the dialogue. She appeals to them not to judge her by the darkness of her complexion (1:6), not to interrupt the couple's lovemaking (2:7; 3:5), and not to tell the man that she is sick with love (5:8). Her brothers, with their misconceptions, provide an opportunity for her to assert her independence of their inhibiting control. The watchmen, the protectors of the city, only briefly encountered the woman, whom they too misunderstood and treated inappropriately. It is apparent that the Song is a celebration of human love, principally from a woman's point of view.

The Tryst

The Song moves from the experience of intense longing to that of blissful enjoyment, and then to longing once more. The woman seeks her absent love and finds him, only to lose him and seek him again. The lovers are separated from each other, joined in an ecstatic embrace, and then apart once again. This alternation between presence and absence, possession and loss, exhilaration and dejection accurately characterizes the ebb and flow of human love with its various combinations of desire, anticipation, and consummation. Everything about this love is mutual (Fox: 305–10). Both the woman and the man move from one emotion to the other. At times she is the initiator, at other times she is reserved. He is variously the object of her search and a forceful suitor. Neither of the lovers has to be cajoled. The tryst is an encounter sought and enjoyed by both lovers.

The trysts take place in several locations: cultivated orchards (2:3; 6:11; 8:5), gardens (4:16–5:1; 6:2), and vineyards (7:12); natural fertile settings (2:16; 6:3; 7:11); and enclosed chambers (2:4; 3:4; 5:2–6; 8:2; cf. Fox: 283–88; Falk: 137–43). Each one of the natural sites is lavish with fruits and the possibility of continuous fertility. In each case the reference to fertility has less to do with progeny, the fruits of sexual fecundity, than with ongoing sensual satisfaction. Not only do these sites promise ample comfort and natural charm, but they provide a modicum of privacy as well. It is not clear whether actual locations are intended or veiled sexual allusions are being made. However, there is no reason to choose one interpretation in favor of the other. Since the Shulammite herself is explicitly referred to as a garden (4:12,15) and the man is compared to a thriving apple tree (2:3), it is possible for these references to be understood both literally and figuratively, thus giving the poems a richness that only multivalent language can boast.

The rooms that lend themselves to lovemaking include a wine house (2:4) and a room in the home of the Shulammite's mother (3:4). Once while she was sleeping, her lover came to her own chamber, but she was slow to admit him and he withdrew (5:2–6). It is quite logical that such rooms as these should be the setting for love. The wine house promotes the image of the vineyard already mentioned. Besides the notion of intoxication, it denotes fruitfulness and maturity, two characteristics of these lovers that have sexual connotations. The room in her mother's home is described as the place where her life began, an allusion to newness but also heavily laden with sexual significance. Finally, the description of the exchange that took place at her own sleeping chamber is quite provocative. It is his intent to enter and consummate their love. Some believe that the passage actually describes coitus (cf. Pope: 519:4–6; Fox: 310–15). The fact that the man seems to have immediate access to her room should be noted. Whether the reference is to an actual room or is a euphemism for genitalia, the only thing that hinders his entry is her delay in opening to him. It is clear that each trysting place is steeped in sexual meaning. Finally, it is the woman who speaks about the site of the rendezvous, not the man. When he does invite her to come away with him, it is to join him. No intimate trysting place is ever mentioned by him (2:10b,13b; 4:8). He appears to be preoccupied with her beauty and his enjoyment of her charms rather than with the details of their meeting.

Another feature of the Song that bespeaks the vibrant surging of the powers of fertility is the season of the year suggested by the poem's vivid imagery. Near Eastern winter, the rainy season, is over; spring has arrived. An abundance of flowers appears; the vines are all in blossom (2:11–15; 6:11). There is a freshness and innocence to nature, just as there is freshness and innocence to the love that has captivated this couple. The man may not have been concerned about the *place* of the tryst, but he is the one who declares that the *time* for love has come (2:11–14). This further suggests that he has interest in when lovemaking occurs, while she is attentive to where it takes place.

The passion of the Shulammite is not indecent, but neither is she demure about it. She enlists both the watchmen and the daughters of Jerusalem in her ardent search for her love. The places of rendezvous may afford the lovers privacy, but they are not secret spots, unknown to others. Although she does not speak explicitly to the men regarding these locations, she is quite open about them to the women (2:4,16; 3:4; 5:2–4; 6:2–3,11; 7:10b–12[9b–11]; 8:2,5b). In fact, the latter may have planned to expedite love by awakening desire in some way, for she pleads with them to allow love to take its natural course without any stimulation or interference (2:7; 3:5; 8:4). However, if by chance they should come upon her lover, they are free to tell him of her longing for him. In fact, she asks them to do this for her (5:8). In this way, the daughters of Jerusalem do play a role in bringing the lovers together, if only an indirect one.

It is clear that this couple has already experienced the pleasures of lovemaking. He has lain on her breast (1:13), been encircled in her embrace (3:4), and been aroused by her (8:5). As already stated, the relationship between the woman and the man is one of mutual desire and enjoyment. Neither one of the lovers nor the couple itself fits a gender-determined stereotype. They are fiercely committed to each other and to no one else. The two use much of the same colorful and provocative imagery to describe each other and the love they share. They have known some form of sexual union (2:16; 6:3) and have both relished the satisfaction that came from it (2:3; 4:10–11). Not only is this clearly stated throughout the Song, but it is implied by the use of metaphors of eating and drinking (1:2,4; 2:3; 4:10–11,16–5:1; 8:2).

The titles of endearment employed in this book are telling. The Shulammite uses straightforward language, consistently calling him "my love." Once she uses "friend" in parallel construction with that endearment, thus signifying the connotation of intimacy carried by the word "friend." He calls her "friend," (1:9,15; 2:2,10b,13; 4:1,7; 5:2; 6:4), "bride" (4:8,9,10,11,12; 5:1), "sister" (4:9,10,12; 5:1,2), and "dove," (2:14; 5:2; 6:9). He further refers to her as "perfect one" (5:2; 6:9), "beautiful one" (2:10b,13), and "noble daughter" (7:2[1]). It is clear that these are all pet names that express the affection that he has for her. Since the poem itself contains no indication that the couple is married or planning to do so, the term "bride" is probably merely an expression of intimacy. "Sister," also a term of endearment, should not be limited to a reference to consanguinity, and "dove" invokes the image of a lovebird. Descriptive phrases are also epithets. "Perfect one" is always in a literary construction with the word "dove" and might be intended as a hendiadys; "beautiful one" addresses the way the man frequently speaks about his love; and "noble daughter" may be a reference to the identification of the woman as a Shulammite (the feminine form of Solomon). It also corresponds to some of the royal imagery found throughout the Song, imagery that can simply allude to the noble character of all human love. All of the language denotes intimacy and admiration.

While the book certainly applauds the glories of lovemaking, more importantly, it celebrates the depth of the commitment shared by the woman and man. Chapter 8:6–7 has been described as the high point of the entire Song. The seals mentioned may refer to apotropaic powers that were often worn around the neck or on the arm. The Shulammite asks that her lover allow her to be for him just such an amulet, a sign of the love that they share. She maintains that their love possesses a force that can easily rival the power of death and Sheol, the place of death. It can even withstand the chaotic primal and flood waters. Neither death nor chaos is a match for the love that joins these two. No power from the netherworld and no treasure from this world can compare with the strength and the value of love.

The Categories of Honor and Shame

The character of female chastity in traditional societies has occupied the interest of anthropologists for some time (Giovannini). It has been associated with institutionalized conceptions of male power and status that constitute the gender-based categories of "honor" and "shame." In the Mediterranean world, these conceptions engendered practices such as female seclusion and the veiling of women, practices that are still evinced in certain cultures today (Deaver; Wikan 1982). The preoccupation with female chastity probably grew out of competition over land and other scarce natural resources (Schneider). Just as the survival of the family or clan was contingent on the quality and measure of water, food, and materials for shelter and protection, so its strength and future was seen as residing in the fertile potential of its women.

Where sexuality is an expression of competition and superiority among men, the fruitfulness of women becomes a resource to protect. This has resulted in male dominance over women. Violating the enclosure of a man's home is comparable to breaching the boundaries of his land. Should a man cross the line of sexual etiquette, he might be in a position to enhance his own status by this challenge to the honor of another, but he and his household are also at risk of some form of reprisal because of the affront. Some believe that the sexuality of women is always in jeopardy and, therefore, always in need of supervision. Since patrilineal inheritance practices within the family or clan are dependent on the legitimacy of offspring, it is imperative that women's sexual activity be monitored. Considerations such as these led to the very strict management of the women (Delaney).

Honor has been described as the convergence of the societal markers of power, gender roles, and respect for those in superior positions (Malina and Neyrey: 41–46). Honor itself is a claim to personal worth in one's own eyes and in the eyes of others. It derives from compliance to the identity conferred upon one by society. It is the basis of one's reputation. Shame is the sensitivity that one has regarding this reputation. It is a positive attitude, concerned with public opinion. It keeps one's behavior in check lest the rules of propriety be transgressed and one's honor be placed in jeopardy. When honor and shame are gender-based, they have different meanings for men and for women. Honor is seen as a male attribute, and shame as a female aspect. For men, shame is a loss of honor; for women, it is the defense of honor. Because such honor is thought to belong to men, a shameless woman dishonors the men of her family. Thus, for the sake of male honor, women were conscientiously protected and controlled.

The men of such a group are responsible for the shame of the women of the group. Depending upon the group, this can take several different forms. In some situations, husbands oversee their wives. In others, brothers exercise significant control over the lives and activities of their sisters. Although honor and shame exhibit themselves in the lives of individuals, control is exercised by the social group. It is the group that determines and regulates propriety and gender-based behavior. It is the group that confers reputation or revokes it. In a very real sense, it is the group that is honored or shamed by the conformity or non-conformity of its members. Social sanctions attached to the behavior of individuals serve the good of the group, both safeguarding traditional mores and tolerating the unfolding of new ones.

More recent ethnographic studies have challenged this gender-based conceptualization of honor and shame (Wikan 1984; Cole: 77–107). They maintain that gender systems are multi-layered and embrace many, often diverse, patterns of interaction between women and men in both the household and the community at large. Apparent ambiguities and contradictions suggest that gender roles and corresponding identities possess a certain degree of fluidity that requires ongoing negotiation between the two sexes. In many anthropological studies, the notion of gender hierarchy has given way to that of gender complementarity (Herzfeld). These studies insist that the only way to understand the social dynamics between women and men is to analyze these dynamics within their own respective socio-cultural context.

The Song of Songs and the Categories of Honor and Shame

Certain features of the Song of Songs appear to conform to the delineation of honor and shame as described above, while other characteristics resist such categorization. For example, the role that the brothers seem to have assumed in the woman's regard (1:6; 8:8) corresponds to customs found in many patriarchal societies, where group cohesion is the primary concern and male consanguines rather than affines are the guardians of female shame. However, the woman in the Song spurns the oversight of her brothers. While it is noteworthy that she acts in this way, it is even more significant that no one and nothing in the Song suggests that she should be censured for such an independent attitude. This is certainly not consistent with the protocol of honor and shame.

Reference to the house of her mother (3:4; 8:2), as well as the easy and frequent exchange the woman has with the daughters of Jerusalem, are familiar features of life in the circumscribed world of women. On the other hand, some features suggest a less restricted context. The woman also has rendezvous with her lover outside of the women's quarters, in a public banquet house (2:4) and in open vineyards (7:12), orchards (2:3; 6:11; 8:5) and fields (2:16; 6:3). Furthermore, her private chamber does not seem to have been secured, for apparently the man has easy access to her room (5:2-6). Although her conversation is primarily with women, it is not restricted to them. She questions the watchmen regarding the whereabouts of her lover (3:3), speaking to them directly and not through some intermediary, and what she says to the daughters of Jerusalem suggests that they might have direct access to her lover (5:8). Behavior such as this does not follow the exacting pattern of female seclusion. Despite this, such deviance is in no way criticized by characters within the Song or by its final editor.

The alluring power of the woman's eyes (4:9; 6:5) concurs with a perception about female seductiveness that has survived to our day (Campbell: 288). Be that as it may, in the Song of Songs the man is as captivating to the woman as she is to him. The attraction, which is definitely strong and sexual, is a mutual attraction. Both the man and the woman extol the physical charms of the other, and revel in the pleasure of their sexual experience. The woman of the Song does not engage in frivolous flirtation. She is self-assured in pursuit of her lover. She fits neither the stereotype of the coquette nor that of the *femme fatale*. Her desire, which is both unabashed and observable, is neither repressed nor manipulated by an overseeing man. Contrary to customs suggested by the honor/shame categories, this assertive woman independently preserves her own honor.

Although the woman makes reference to public opinion (8:1), she does not seem to be intimidated by it. Nor does she appear to consider her unaccompanied nocturnal search of the city behavior of which she should be ashamed. Her true identity may have been mistaken by the watchmen, but the attitude of the Song insinuates that it was their behavior that was unseemly and not that of the woman. Her conduct seems understandable and quite acceptable, even though it does not conform to the patterns associated with honor and shame.

It cannot be denied that the categories of honor and shame provide a framework for comprehending certain features of the Song, but these features can all be understood in other ways. For instance, the harsh treatment that the woman endured at the hands of the watchmen (5:7) might be explained as the punishment meted out to a woman who violated her society's seclusion taboo. However, the suggestion that such beating was the kind of treatment afforded a prostitute (Pope: 527–8) is not convincing. Another example of the usefulness of the categories of honor and shame is the mention of the garden as enclosed (4:12) and as belonging to the man (5:1; 6:2). Some commentators regard these references as allusions to female seclusion with exclusive access only by certain privileged males. This is not a totally satisfying interpretation, for the man in the Song is neither a legitimate member of her family of origin nor is he her husband. In this instance, exclusive access flows from the preferential character of love. Only her lover is admitted into the enclosure.

The general tenor of the Song of Songs throws into question most of the characteristics associated with the notions of honor and shame. There is no underlying concern for male power and status and, consequently, there is no interest in controlling what might threaten it. The sexual activity of the woman is neither suppressed nor supervised. The passionate union of the woman and man is sought for the mutual pleasure that it promises and not for the purposes of procreation and the heirs that it might yield. Furthermore, the lovers are not married, nor do they appear to be betrothed. In other words, the patriarchal concern of safeguarding the chastity of the woman for the sake of progeny is not evident here.

What then can be said about the categories of honor and shame as heuristic models for interpretation? Presuming that they do represent actual societal patterns, the social relations depicted in the Song of Songs are notably uncommon. This point raises several questions of an historical nature. Might the Song illustrate behavior that was peculiar to a particular stratum of society rather than conduct that was established as standard? If this is the case, which class is represented here? Is it the peasant class (cf. 1:6, vine-dressers), which, because of financial necessity, was unable to conform to social propriety? Or is it the royalty (cf. 1:12), which frequently claimed exemption from general norms? When all is said and done, the identification of the social class portrayed in the Song of Songs does not explain why a book that narrates such unconventional behavior should have attained the canonical status it came to enjoy.

It is remarkable that a society such as ancient Israel, which appears to have had such a strict sexual code of ethics, at least for women, would have produced or preserved a piece of literature such as the Song of Songs. This unique composition neither censors the unrestricted aggressiveness of the woman nor condemns sexual behavior outside of marriage or betrothal. With the exception of the watchmen, none of the characters conforms to the gender-based models advanced by the concepts of honor and shame. The fact that the woman of the Song is the only unmediated female voice in scripture, the thoughts of other biblical women being conveyed through the voices of narrators (Weems: 156), along with the claim that only a woman could so accurately describe female impassioned aspirations, have led many to propose female authorship for the book. Should this be the case, it still does not explain how the Song gained acceptance and even canonical status within a society that was clearly patriarchal in its socio-political organization and androcentric in its bias. It is precisely its peculiar and even unorthodox character that down through the ages persuaded commentators that the book's real meaning lay in its symbolic rather than in its literal sense. The present-day movement away from this interpretive position has brought the modern interpreter face-to-face with the enigmatic character of the relationship between the woman and the man depicted in the lyrics of the Song of Songs.

One would expect that the overt sexual character of the Song of Songs would lend itself to an analysis according to the gender-defined categories of honor and shame. It does not. In fact, the contrary is true. A close reading of the poems reveals social relationships that are anomalous, if the honor/shame model is the norm. Does this divergence highlight the idiosyncratic nature of this biblical book, or might it suggest that the etic model must be more flexible when applied to an emic world? If the sexual relationship depicted here is more characteristic than previously believed, then the Song of Songs might serve as an interpretive key to unlocking the revelatory possibilities of other texts.

Works Consulted

Alter, Robert
    1981   *The Art of Biblical Narrative.* New York: Basic Books.

Beattie, John
    1964   *Other Cultures: Aims, Methods, and Achievements in Social Anthropology.* New York: The Free Press.

Boas, Franz
    1955   *Race, Language, and Culture.* New York: Macmillan.

Campbell, J. K.
    1964   *Honor, Family, and Patronage: A Study of Institutions and Moral Values in a Greek Mountain Community.* Oxford: Clarendon Press.

Cole, Sally
    1991   *Women of the Praia.* Princeton: Princeton University Press.

Deaver, Sherri
1980 "The Contemporary Saudi Woman." Pp. 19–42 in *The World of Women*. Ed. Erika Bourguignon. PRAEGER Special Studies. New York: J. F. Bergin.

Delaney, Carol
1987 "Seeds of Honor, Fields of Shame." Pp.35–48 in *Honor and Shame and the Unity of the Mediterranean*. Ed. David D. Gilmore. Washington D.C.: American Anthropological Society.

Durkheim, Emile
1961 *The Elementary Forms of Religious Life*. New York: Collier.

Elliot, M. Timothea
1989 *The Literary Unity of the Canticle*. European University Series 23. Bern: Peter Lang.

Exum, J. Cheryl
1973 "A Literary and Structural Analysis of the Song of Songs." *ZAW* 85:47–79.

Falk, Marcia
1990 *The Song of Songs*. San Francisco: Harper.

Fox, Michael V.
1985 *The Song of Songs and the Ancient Egyptian Love Songs*. Madison: University of Wisconsin Press.

Geertz, Clifford
1973 *The Interpretation of Cultures*. New York: Harper Torch Books.
1988 *Works and Lives: The Anthropologist as Author*. Stanford, CA: Stanford University Press.

Gilmore, David D., ed.
1987 *Honor and Shame and the Unity of the Mediterranean*. Washington D.C.: American Anthropological Society.

Giovannini, Maureen, J.
1987 "Female Chastity Code in the Circum-Mediterranean: Comparative Perspectives." Pp.61–74 in *Honor and Shame and the Unity of the Mediterranean*. Ed. David D. Gilmore. Washington D.C.: American Anthropological Society.

Gordis, Robert
1974 *The Song of Songs and Lamentations* (revised and augmented edition). New York: KTAV.

Harris, Marvin
1976 "History and Significance of the Emic/Etic Distinction." *Annual Review of Anthropology* 5:329–50.

Herzfeld, M.
　1986　"Within and Without: The Category of 'Female' in the Ethnography of Modern Greece." Pp. 215–33 in *Gender and Power in Rural Greece*. Ed. J. Dubisch. Princeton: Princeton University Press.

Jackson, Michael
　1989　*Paths Toward a Clearing: Radical Empiricism and Ethnographic Inquiry*. Bloomington/Indianapolis: Indiana University Press.

Jorgensen, Danny L.
　1989　*Participant Observation: A Methodology for Human Studies*. Newbury Park, CA: Sage Publications.

Kroeber, A. L.
　1952　*The Nature of Culture*. Chicago: University of Chicago Press.

Landsberger, Franz
　1954　"Poetic Units Within the Song of Songs." *JBL* 73:203–216.

Leach, Edmund
　1976　*Culture and Communication*. Cambridge: Cambridge University Press.
　1983　*Structuralist Interpretations of Biblical Myth*. Cambridge: Cambridge University Press.

Lewis, I. M.
　1976　*Social Anthropology in Perspective*. Harmondsworth: Penguin Books.

Malina, Bruce
　1981　*The New Testament World: Insights from Cultural Anthropology*. Atlanta: John Knox.

Malina, Bruce & Jerome H. Neyrey
　1991　"Honor and Shame in Luke-Acts." Pp. 25–65 in *The Social World of Luke-Acts*. Ed. Jerome H. Neyrey. Peabody, MA: Hendrickson.

Murphy, Roland E.
　1981　*Wisdom Literature*. Grand Rapids: Eerdsman.
　1990　*The Song of Songs*. Hermeneia. Minneapolis: Fortress.

Okely, Judith and H. Callaway
　1992　*Anthropology and Autobiography*. ASA Monographs 29. London: Routledge.

Peristiany, J. G., ed.
　1966　*Honor and Shame: The Values of Mediterranean Society*. Chicago: University of Chicago Press.

Pope, Marvin H.
　1977　*The Song of Songs*. The Anchor Bible. Garden City, NY: Doubleday.

Pouget, Guillaume & Jean Guitton
　1934　*The Canticle of Canticles*. Tr. Joseph L. Lilly. New York: Declan X. McMullen.

Robert, Andre, Raymond Tournay, & Andre Feuillet
    1963   *Le Cantique des Cantiques*. Paris: Etudes Bibliques.

Schneider, Jane
    1971   "Of Vigilance and Virgins." *Ethnology* 10:1–24.

Trible, Phyllis
    1978   *God and the Rhetoric of Sexuality*. Overtures to Biblical Theology. Philadelphia: Fortress.

Weems, Renita
    1992   "Song of Songs." Pp. 156–60 in *The Women's Bible Commentary*. Eds. Carol A. Newsom & Sharon H. Ringe. London: SPCK.

Wikan, Unni
    1982   *Behind the Veil in Arabia: Women in Oman*. Baltimore: Johns Hopkins.
    1984   "Shame and Honour: A Contestable Pair." *Man* 19:635–52.

Worgul, G.
    1979   "Anthropological Consciousness and Biblical Theology." *BTB* 9:3–12.

"RETURN TO YAHWEH": HONOR AND SHAME IN JOEL

Ronald A. Simkins

ABSTRACT

This paper interprets Joel's call for the people to return to Yahweh (2:12–14) from the perspective of the honor/shame model derived from recent studies of the cultural anthropology of the Mediterranean peoples. Prior scholarship has employed a covenant model with the four-fold pattern of sin-judgment-repentance-blessing in order to interpret this passage as a call to repentance. This covenant model, however, has little correspondence with the biblical text. It fails to answer the fundamental question raised by the model: What sins of the people had brought upon them the natural catastrophe as a sign of God's judgment? In contrast, the honor/shame model corresponds with both the vocabulary and the emphasis of the text. According to this model, Joel's call for the people to return to Yahweh is interpreted as a summons for the people to honor Yahweh by demonstrating their allegiance to him with acts of mourning appropriate to their suffering.

I. JOEL'S SILENCE ON THE SINS OF THE PEOPLE

According to the text of Joel, the people of Judah had experienced an unparalleled ecological and economic catastrophe. A severe locust plague had destroyed the grain and the fruit harvest to the extent that even the temple lacked sufficient provisions to maintain the practice of the cult. Moreover, the text of Joel suggests that this catastrophe was compounded further by a drought and the possible onslaught of an enemy invasion. To the people of Judah who had suffered from this catastrophe, the prophet Joel holds out a message of hope:

> But even now—oracle of Yahweh:
> Return to me with your whole heart,
>   with fasting, weeping, and lamentation.
>
> Rend your heart, and not your garments;
>   return to Yahweh your God
>
> For he is gracious and compassionate
>   long forbearing and abundant in kindness,
>   and relents from evil.
>
> Who knows whether he will again relent
>   and leave behind him a blessing,

> the grain offering and wine libation for Yahweh your God.
> (Joel 2:12–14)

In anticipation of God's deliverance of the people from the natural catastrophe that is afflicting them, Joel calls the people of Judah to return to Yahweh. Scholars have interpreted this passage within the context of a covenant model. A model is simply a conceptual map used to organize diverse data, in this case, from the text of Joel, into a meaningful pattern (Carney: 1–11). The covenant model, derived from the biblical, especially deuteronomistic and prophetic, literature, is based on the repeated pattern of sin-judgment-repentance-blessing. By reading chapters 1–2 from the perspective of this model, most biblical scholars have assumed that the people of Judah had sinned against God, and that the natural catastrophe itself was the sign of God's judgment. The "return to Yahweh" has been interpreted accordingly to mean that if the people repent of their transgressions against God, the catastrophe will be averted, and, instead of devastation and judgment, the people will experience Yahweh's blessing.

This interpretation of the book of Joel, however, is problematic. Based on the covenant model, 2:12–14 has usually been characterized as a "call to repentance." But although this is a typical and straightforward genre of the prophetic literature, Joel's use of this form of speech occasions numerous questions: What does "return to Yahweh" mean in this context? From what or whom should the people return? What is the condition of the people that necessitates their return? In fact, nowhere in the book does Joel describe the people's transgressions or declare God's judgment on them. One recent commentator cynically articulates the frustration that all interpreters of the book of Joel inevitably face:

> In Joel there isn't a clue as to what specific act or event has caused destruction to come upon the land, though clearly no outside force has victimized man. Man is asked to supply the remedy, so presumably he is the cause. He is bidden to fast, to gather for prayer, to cry unto the Lord. What transgressions of his have brought this plague of locusts? None is stated. What is implied in the injunctions to weep, fast, and cry unto the Lord is that there hasn't been enough of such activities. These aren't sinners in the hands of an angry God; they are people in the hands of a megalomaniac God. (Shapiro: 201)

What transgressions had brought the natural catastrophe upon the people? Unlike all the other biblical prophets, at no place in the text does Joel delineate why, or from what, the people should repent. Evidently, it was sufficient for Joel's purpose merely to call the people to return to Yahweh, and consequently, to offer the hope that the terrible catastrophe — the day of Yahweh — would be averted. Perhaps this was sufficient for the people, Joel's original audience, as well. After all, in the midst of suffering the struggle for deliverance often overrides any need for justification. But modern commentators have not been so content to embrace Joel's silence on the otherwise apparent sins of the people.

It is understandable why commentators demand further clarification with regard to the people's sins. We want to know why the people had suffered so that we can justify the prophet's call to repentance. Far too often we have had to confront the reality that innocent people suffer at the hand of nature, whether it be earthquakes, hurricanes or tornadoes, droughts or floods, famines, or viruses. All of these afflictions exact an immeasurable toll on innocent human lives. Such disasters are attributed to fate, to human negligence, or to the unpredictable powers of nature, but not to God, at least not to *our* God. A righteous and just God would not whimsically punish innocent people. Therefore, for Joel to interpret the natural catastrophe as Yahweh's judgment on the people, without at the same time ascribing to them guilt or sin, is intolerable with respect to our understanding of God. If Joel calls the people to return to Yahweh, surely they had sinned! Like Eliphaz, Bildad, and Zophar, we must search out and identify that sin. Numerous scholars have thus presented elaborate interpretations based on the covenant model in order to explain Joel's call to repentance in light of some specific sin of the people.

Wolff, for example, argues that Joel's summons to return to Yahweh was a call in the deuteronomistic tradition for the people to listen anew to the prophetic word, and specifically to the prophetic announcement of the day of Yahweh (1975; 1977:48–49). The people of Judah, and the temple community in particular, had begun to pride themselves on their fulfillment of the Torah. The temple community no longer felt that the prophetic word was necessary, for through their cultic worship and adherence to the Torah they believed that they had secured their own salvation. But rather than trusting in the functioning cultus of Jerusalem, Joel calls the people to wait for God to act according to the prophetic word as the one who would come in judgment and establish himself as lord of the nations (1977:48–53).

On a similar course, Redditt suggests that the message of Joel was directed against the cultic establishment. According to his interpretation, Joel was critical of Jerusalem's priests and elders because in the midst of catastrophe they had abdicated their leadership of the cult. The sin underlying Joel's call to repentance is ascribed to the religious leaders alone, for they had failed to keep the cultus functioning. Joel thus called for these religious leaders to assume their proper position in the administration of the cult (235–36).

A different approach to the sin underlying Joel's call to repentance is taken by Ahlström. After placing the book within a covenantal context, he claims that the phrase *subu 'aday*, "return to me," indicates that the people had been worshiping other gods, for it demands by its very nature that the people return to no other god than Yahweh. Joel's emphasis on the people's repentance by means of a correct cult—fasting, weeping, lamentation—also signals for Ahlström that their sin consisted in the practice of a wrong cult. "If the cult had been wrong, this means, according to the prophet, that the people practiced some other cult, and this must necessarily have been directed to some other god, because we have no right to believe that there was a godless cult in the temple of Jerusalem" (26). According to Ahlström, Joel was simply standing within the tradition of the pre-exilic prophets who repeatedly condemned the people for participating in a syncretistic cult (26–28).

Each of these interpretations of Joel's call to repentance attempts to justify the use of the covenant model for interpreting the book of Joel by clarifying the sin of the people. The value of any interpretive model is determined by whether or not it can account for the data of a given text within a meaningful, socially plausible framework. Does the model adequately explain the relationship of the diverse elements of the text? Although each interpretation, derived from the covenant model, does answer the crucial question of why Joel called the people to return to Yahweh, none can marshal substantial evidence from the text in support. On the one hand, the readings of the text based on these interpretations are at best conjectural, attempting to render explicit what Joel was content to leave implicit. On the other hand, the text itself argues against these interpretations. Nowhere does Joel criticize the religious establishment. Nowhere does he accuse the people of worshiping other gods or practicing a wrong cult. Rather, on these issues Joel is silent.

Perhaps Joel's silence with regard to the sin of the people should be taken at face value. Perhaps the people had committed no transgressions against Yahweh, and Joel's message to them served as a theodicy by placing their suffering within a meaningful frame of reference. Repeatedly, Joel places the natural catastrophe within the context of earlier prophetic traditions, including the day of Yahweh (1:15; 2:1–2, 11; 3:3–5), the enemy from the north (2:3–9, 20), Yahweh's defeat of the nations (4:4–17), and the restoration of the land (2:21–24; 4:18). It is important to note that nowhere does Joel address the people from the perspective of Yahweh's wrath. Nowhere does he declare Yahweh's judgment on the people (Bergler: 339–40). Emphasis of the text instead is placed on the people's response to the catastrophe and Yahweh's promised redemption.

What then should be the people's response to the catastrophe? What does it mean for the people to return to Yahweh? Clearly, "return to Yahweh" does not always mean "repent from your sins." For example, compare the use of this injunction in the context of Second Isaiah's message of redemption:

> Remember these things, O Jacob,
> Israel, that you are my servant;
>
> I formed you, you are my servant,
> Israel, you are not forgotten by me.
>
> I wiped away your rebellions like a mist,
> and your sins like a cloud;
> return to me for I redeemed you.
>
> Shout with joy, O heavens, for Yahweh acted,
> shout, O depths of the earth;
>
> Break forth in singing, O mountains,
> forests with all its trees;
>
> For Yahweh redeemed Jacob
> and will display his glory in Israel.
>
> (Isaiah 44:21–23)

Although Second Isaiah explicitly refers to the people's past sins, the prophet is not saying, "Repent from your sins so that Yahweh will redeem you." According to this passage, Yahweh's forgiveness of sins and redemption are not conditional. God had already forgiven and redeemed his people. What is at issue for Second Isaiah, and that which forms the core of his message, is not Yahweh's forgiveness of his people but the people's response to God's redemption. Similarly, Joel's call for the people to return may anticipate God's forthcoming redemption rather than signal the people's prior or current sins.

If no sins of the people of Judah had brought on the natural catastrophe, and Joel's oracles in turn were not a message of judgment, then the covenant model cannot adequately elucidate the text of Joel. There are too few correspondences between the model and the text. It is the thesis of this article that a more appropriate model for understanding Joel's call for the people to return to Yahweh is the honor/shame model derived from recent studies of the cultural anthropology of the Mediterranean peoples. Unlike the covenant model, the honor/shame model has frequent and explicit correspondences with the text itself. This should become apparent from a survey of the textual evidence.

II. THE SHAME OF THE PEOPLE

The book of Joel is set against the background of a catastrophe which is described with the images of a locust plague, a drought, and an enemy invasion. I have argued in detail elsewhere that all of these images can be accounted for by a severe locust plague which devastated Judah over the period of two agricultural seasons (Simkins: 101–69). The locusts are described with military metaphors as an enemy army invading the land: Like an overpowering foe, the locusts march undeterred, devouring all vegetation in their path. Similarly, the accompanying drought imagery is used to dramatize the effects of the locust plague: The defoliated trees and vines and the consumed fields and pastures appear as if they had been parched by a drought. In addition to the ecological destruction, the locust plague caused harsh economic consequences, for with the loss of the harvest, the people were deprived of their primary form of subsistence. The shortage of foodstuffs even resulted in the suspension of the temple cult because there were no provisions for the daily sacrifices—the grain offering and wine libation.

To those who had suffered from this ecological and economic catastrophe, Joel addressed a series of four oracles (1:5–14), which can be characterized as "calls to lamentation" (Wolff 1964; 1977:21–22), in order to provide an appropriate liturgical structure for the emotions which the people had experienced. Of the emotions expressed, shame plays a prominent role. The third oracle reads:

> Stand ashamed,[1] O tillers of the soil!
>   Wail, O vine dressers,
> on account of the wheat and barley, for the harvest of the field perished—
> The vine is dried up,
>   and the fig tree withered;
> The pomegranate, even the date palm and apple tree,
>   all the trees of the field are dried up—
> for joy has been put to shame by the nations.
>   (Joel 1:11–12)

The devastation caused by the locust plague was a source of shame for the people. In this particular oracle the prophet simply singles out the farmers and the vine dressers because their livelihood had been destroyed by the locusts.

In the final line of this oracle Joel further emphasizes the shame of the people. The interpretation of this line, however, is ambiguous. The verb הֹבִישׁ can be interpreted as a Hiphil from either בּוֹשׁ, "to be ashamed," or יָבֵשׁ, "to be dry." Most scholars have derived הֹבִישׁ from יָבֵשׁ; the last line of the oracle is generally translated, "Indeed, joy has withered from the sons of men," or in some similar fashion. But this interpretation is improbable in this context for the Hiphil of יָבֵשׁ is never used with the

---

[1] Stuart translates הֹבִישׁוּ as "wilt," as if it were derived from יָבֵשׁ, "to be dry." He then interprets it as a pun referring to the people's despair (237, 243). Stuart is certainly correct that a pun is intended, but it is more likely that the pun concerns the farmers' shame: Because the plants and the trees are dried up (הֹבִישׁוּ from יָבֵשׁ), the farmers are ashamed (הֹבִישׁוּ from בּוֹשׁ).

meaning "to be dried up *from*." On the other hand, the root בּוֹשׁ is used idiomatically with *min* to mean "to be put to shame *by*." Compare the use of this idiom in the following texts:

> For you will be put to shame by (-מ תֵבֹשׁוּ)[2] the oaks in which you delight,
> and you will be disgraced by the gardens that you choose.
> (Isa 1:29)
> How very frivolously you act
>   to change your way;
> Indeed, by Egypt you will be shamed (-מ תֵבֹשִׁי)
>   as you were shamed by (-מ בֹּשְׁתְּ) Assyria.
> (Jer 2:36)

> Everyone is ignorant of kno7wledge;
> every smith is put to shame by (-מ הֹבִישׁ) his idol,
> for his image is false and has no breath.
> (Jer 10:14 = 51:17)

The verb in v. 12, then, should be interpreted from בּוּשׁ and translated accordingly. But how was joy put to shame by the nations?

Many scholars have assumed that the Hebrew synonyms for joy refer to an internal emotional pleasure, and according to this understanding it is difficult to imagine how joy can be put to shame. In several recent publications, however, Gary Anderson argues convincingly that the Hebrew terms for joy are linked with specific, concrete activities. According to his analysis, the term "joy" in the Semitic languages,

> is not so much a general term of emotional pleasure, but rather a term which connotes particular pleasures associated with the observation of specific rituals. In particular, the pleasures that are most characteristic of the experience of joy are those which stand in typological contrast to those of mourning. Thus, just as mourning consists of fasting, rending the garments, putting dust on the head, and sexual continence, so the experience of joy included eating and drinking, putting on festal attire, anointing oneself with oil and bathing, and sexual union (1989:133).

Emotion and behavior have a reciprocal relationship in the world of the Bible and the ancient Near East in general. Emotion is the product of behavior; the ritual behavior elicits the appropriate emotion. Behavior in turn limits and defines emotion by externalizing and objectifying it. Moreover, Anderson demonstrates that the acts of joy and mourning have a correlation with the presence of God within the life of the individual and the community. In other words, acts of joy are the proper response to the presence of God, whereas God's absence expects various acts of mourning (1991).

---

[2] Reading תֵבֹשׁוּ with the majority of scholars instead of יָבֹשׁוּ of the MT.

In the context of Joel, joy is specifically associated with the pleasures of offering the daily sacrifices which the locust plague had brought to an end. Due to the absence of God in delivering his people, joy should be replaced by mourning.

> Gird yourselves and mourn, O priests.
>   Wail, O ministers of the altar.
> Come, spend the night in sackcloth, O ministers of God,
> for grain and wine are withheld from the temple of God . . .
> Is not the food cut off before our eyes,
>   joy and gladness from the temple of our God.
>   (Joel 1:13, 16)

The joy that is put to shame, then, is best interpreted as a metonym for the people who participate in the daily sacrifices. The people who no longer were able to experience the joy of the grain and wine offerings had been put to shame by the nations. The phrase translated "nations" is simply בְּנֵי אָדָם. Although this idiom denotes humankind in general, Joel uses it in contrast to the בְּנֵי סִיּוֹן (2:23). The בְּנֵי אָדָם are simply those outside of the community of Yahweh, the בְּנֵי סִיּוֹן, whose judgment the community deemed important. This claim is supported from the text in 2:17, for in that context Joel calls the priests to pray as follows:

> Spare, O Yahweh, your people!
> Do not appoint your inheritance as a disgrace, to be taunted by the nations;
> why should they say among the peoples, "Where
>   is their God?"
>   (Joel 2:17)

The absence of God within the community, as attested by the devastation of the locusts, and as judged by the nations, was a source of shame for the people of Judah.

The idea that the people of Judah found their catastrophic plight shameful is further attested in the salvation oracle in 2:18–27. Because Yahweh is jealous for his land and has compassion on his people, he will destroy the locusts, so that Judah is not a disgrace among the nations. He will restore the agricultural bounty of the land. The trees and vines will bear their fruit, and the fields will produce an abundance of grain. The people will again be able to rejoice and be glad; they will again be able to offer the daily sacrifices. There will be plenty of food to eat so that the people will never be ashamed again. In the final verse of the oracle, Joel emphasizes the purpose of Yahweh's salvation:

> Then you will know that I am in the midst of Israel,
> and I, Yahweh, am your God, and there is no other;
> and my people will never be ashamed again.
>   (Joel 2:27)

The locust plague had been interpreted as a sign of Yahweh's absence, bringing shame on his people. But Yahweh's destruction of the locusts and restoration of the land will demonstrate Yahweh's presence among his people. Their mourning will be turned into joy, and they will no longer be ashamed before the nations.

III. Honor and Shame and the Interpretation of Joel

From this brief textual survey, it should be clear that the shame of the people plays some factor in Joel's call for the people to return to Yahweh. At the very least, the return of the people to Yahweh will result in the removal of their shame. But does shame play a more prominent role? The textual evidence itself is ambiguous, for it assumes crucial knowledge from the readers, knowledge about, for example, the meaning of shame, the importance of mourning rituals, and the significance of the people's perception of the nations. Although this knowledge has been lost to antiquity, comparative studies of similar cultures can suggest a plausible body of knowledge from which to understand this text. In particular, the honor/shame model, based on the dominant values shared by most Mediterranean cultures, can provide an appropriate framework for interpretation. Based on this model, I propose that shame plays a central role in the text of Joel, and that the shame of the people is in fact the occasion for Joel's call for the people to return to Yahweh.

In Mediterranean cultures honor and shame are the dominant values determinative of a person's identity and social status (Malina: 25–50; Malina and Neyrey). Honor can be defined as "the value of a person in his own eyes, but also in the eyes of his society. It is his estimation of his own worth, his claim to pride, but it is also the acknowledgment of that claim, his excellence recognized by society, his right to pride" (Pitt-Rivers: 1). Honor is the basis of a person's reputation and social position; it is an indication of one's power and precedence in the society. This social aspect is the essential feature of the Mediterranean value of honor because it is in the public arena where claims to honor are made. It is public opinion that determines a person's reputation, for a person who claims honor that is not publicly recognized claims only vanity. But through the offering of precedence, and through demonstrations of respect, others grant a person's claim to honor and secure his self-image.

Honor can be ascribed from birth or privilege—that is, one inherits the honor of one's parents or is endowed with honor from persons in power—but more often, honor is achieved through the confrontation of challenge and riposte with one's peers (Bourdieu: 99–117). Traditional Mediterranean societies are thus frequently characterized by anthropologists as agonistic societies. These are societies in which intense competition among social equals is a way of life, and this competition is often perceived as a battle for personal honor or family reputation. On the positive side, the competition for honor and reputation provides a socially acceptable outlet for aggressions, diminishing the possibility of feuds or wars. However, on the other side, it produces a definite tension which permeates individual and group interactions:

> Neighbors are on the one hand perceived as dangerous rivals, but they are also recognized as sources of economic, social, and sexual needs, and as being necessary for the confirmation of personal status. This ambivalence of dependency *vs* opposition sets up an unusually powerful tension in interpersonal relations in Mediterranean communities. This tension is often resolved publicly through norms of superficial cordiality and ritualized reciprocity. But antagonisms remain in repressed form, finding expression in misanthropic perceptions and suspicions, and in other sublimated hostilities (Gilmore: 189).

Honor is a limited commodity. Through successful challenge and riposte, one gains honor at the loss of another's honor. Shame is the result of the failure to defend one's honor, or the public denial of one's claim to honor.

Within the public arena the values of honor and shame have both an individual and corporate dimension. A person's identity is defined not only in terms of his own personal honor but also in terms of the collective honor of the group to which he belongs. Unlike the individualism of Western societies, Mediterranean societies are characterized by group consciousness (Robinson):

> The Western conception of the person as a bounded, unique, more or less integrated motivational and cognitive universe, a dynamic center of awareness, emotion, judgment, and action organized into a distinctive whole and set contrastively both against other such wholes and against its social and natural background, is, however incorrigible it may seem to us, a rather peculiar idea within the context of the world's cultures (Geertz: 225).

The individual depends upon the perception of others for his self-identity, his self-worth (Malina: 128–30). Honor becomes accordingly the "basis of the ethic appropriate to an individual who always sees himself through the eyes of others, who has need of others in order to exist, because his self-image is inseparable from the image of himself that he receives back from others" (Bourdieu: 136). Consequently, the actions of one member in the group affect the reputation of the whole group. Similarly, all members share individually in the honor or shame of the group.

All cultures in the Mediterranean share the common values of honor and shame. The people of all these cultures are concerned about their honor, but each culture varies on what in fact is honorable or shameful. That which is honorable or shameful is often local, variable, and ad hoc

(Davis: 23; Herzfeld; Malina and Neyrey: 26–27). Any application of the honor/shame model, therefore, must take the local context into account.

In most Mediterranean cultures, the quest for honor and the avoidance of shame occurs within a familial context. Brother is pitted against brother, or more frequently one family competes against another. The expression of honor or shame in the Bible is frequently set within this familial context, as some of the articles in this volume demonstrate. But in the Bible the language of honor and shame is also applied to international relations. The honor or shame of the people of God depends on their status as a nation in relation to their neighbors. For example, the destruction of Judah, particularly at the hand of another nation, is repeatedly described as a source of shame (Jer 3:3, 25; 9:19; Lam 5:1; Neh 1:3; 2:17). Moreover, the absence of God is also considered to be shameful to the people (Mic 3:7; Jer 48:13), for this demonstrates their vulnerability or weakness before the nations.

In the book of Joel, that which is shameful is the devastation of the land and destruction of the agriculture (compare Ezek 36:30). Such a plight is shameful because it makes a mockery of Judah's claim to be the people of Yahweh and to enjoy the benefits of loyalty to him. If Yahweh was their God, and if the people had properly honored him through obedience to his commands, then it was incumbent upon Yahweh to bless and protect them (compare Prov 3:9–10). The devastation caused by the locust plague, however, was public evidence against such a claim to honor. Thus, the people of Judah were shamed before the nations.

Within this social context Joel issued his call for the people to return to Yahweh. The literary context of this call suggests that returning to Yahweh entails, at least, fasting, weeping, and lamentation. Elsewhere in the text Joel calls the people, and the priests in particular, to lament, to mourn, to put on sackcloth, to sanctify a fast, and to assemble at the temple and cry to Yahweh. Evidently, the people and priests had been participating in none of these rites. Perhaps Joel's call for the people to return to Yahweh is simply a summons for the people to engage in the acts of mourning appropriate to their plight, and so to honor Yahweh by demonstrating their allegiance to him.

If the people of Judah had been shamed before the nations, as the text indicates, what would have been their response? The universal response to shame is to hide oneself, to cover that which has been exposed to shame (Schneider: 29–39), but what would this entail for the people of Judah? The text asserts that the people's participation in the daily sacrifices had been put to shame by the nations. Ritual participation in the cult of Yahweh was the people's public claim to honor. It was an act of the people's devotion to their God, and a claim to be the benefactors of God's blessing. But the people's claim to honor was empty. Yahweh did not spare them the devastation caused by the locust plague, and so they were shamed before the eyes of the nations. Their participation in the cult of Yahweh compounded their shame, as symbolized by their inability to keep the daily sacrifices going. Not only had God brought devastation, and consequently, shame, upon the people, but the means by which they demonstrated their faithfulness to God had ceased. In response, the people simply withdrew from the public practice of the cult (compare Mal 1:13).

The use of this honor/shame model for interpreting Joel accounts for the data of the text within a meaningful frame of reference. It leaves unanswered the question of the people's sin, but the text itself is silent on this issue. Joel's concern is elsewhere — namely, with the people's response to the catastrophe. Therefore, the honor/shame model supplies an appropriate framework for understanding Joel's call for the people to return to Yahweh. The people of Judah had suffered an ecological and economic catastrophe caused by the infestation of a severe locust plague. With the grain and fruit crops destroyed, and the pastures consumed as if scorched by fire, the struggle for subsistence must have dominated the attention of the people. The ritual practice of the cult, having been a reminder of their shame, was easily abandoned. To these people Joel addressed a message of hope: Return to Yahweh by honoring him with the appropriate acts of mourning, and Yahweh will restore your honor. Yahweh will destroy the locusts and restore the land so that the people will never be ashamed again.

WORKS CITED

Ahlström, Gösta W.
    1971   *Joel and the Temple Cult of Jerusalem*. VTSup 21. Leiden: E. J. Brill.

Anderson, Gary A.
    1989   "Celibacy or Consummation in the Garden? Reflections on Early Jewish and Christian Interpretations of the Garden of Eden." *HTR* 82:121–48.
    1991   *A Time to Mourn, A Time to Dance: The Expression of Grief and Joy in Israelite Religion*. Philadelphia: University of Pennsylvania Press.

Bergler, Siegfried
    1988   *Joel als Schriftinterpret*. Beiträge zur Erforschung des Alten Testaments und des antiken Judentums 16. Frankfort am Main: Peter Lang.

Bourdieu, Pierre
 1979   *Algeria 1960*. Cambridge: Cambridge University Press.

Carney, Thomas F.
 1975   *The Shape of the Past: Models and Antiquity*. Lawrence, KS: Coronado.

Davis, John
 1987   "Family and State in the Mediterranean." Pp. 22–34 in *Honor and Shame and the Unity of the Mediterranean*. American Anthropological Association Special Publication 22. Ed. D. D. Gilmore. Washington, D.C.: American Anthropological Association.

Geertz, Clifford
 1976   "'From a Native's Point of View': On the Nature of Anthropological Understanding." Pp. 221–37 in *Meaning in Anthropology*. Ed. K. H. Basso and H. A. Selby. Albuquerque: University of New Mexico Press.

Gilmore, David D.
 1982   "Anthropology of the Mediterranean Area." *Annual Review of Anthropology* 11:175–205.

Herzfeld, Michael
 1987   "'As in Your Own House:' Hospitality, Ethnography, and the Stereotype of Mediterranean Society." Pp. 75–89 in *Honor and Shame and the Unity of the Mediterranean*. American Anthropological Association Special Publication 22. Ed. D. D. Gilmore. Washington, D.C.: American Anthropological Association.

Malina, Bruce J.
 1981   *The New Testament World: Insights from Cultural Anthropology*. Atlanta: John Knox.
 1989   "Dealing with Biblical (Mediterranean) Characters: A Guide for U.S. Consumers." *BTB* 19:127–41.

Malina, Bruce J. and Jerome H. Neyrey
 1991   "Honor and Shame in Luke-Acts: Pivotal Values of the Mediterranean World." Pp. 25–65 in *The Social World of Luke-Acts: Models for Interpretation*. Ed. J. H. Neyrey. Peabody, MA: Hendrickson.

Pitt-Rivers, Julian
 1977   *The Fate of Shechem or the Politics of Sex: Essays in the Anthropology of the Mediterranean*. Cambridge: Cambridge University Press.

Redditt, Paul D.
 1986   "The Book of Joel and Peripheral Prophecy." *CBQ* 48:225–40.

Robinson, H. Wheeler
 1936   "The Hebrew Conception of Corporate Personality." Pp. 49–62 in *Werden und Wesen des Alten Testaments*. BZAW 66. Ed. P. Voltz, et al. Berlin: A. Töpelmann.

Schneider, Carl D.
 1977   *Shame, Exposure and Privacy*. Boston: Beacon.

Shapiro, H.
- 1987 "Joel." Pp. 197–209 in *Congregation: Contemporary Writers Read the Jewish Bible*. Ed. D. Rosenberg. San Diego: Harcourt Brace Jovanovich.

Simkins, Ronald A.
- 1991 *Yahweh's Activity in History and Nature in the Book of Joel*. Ancient Near Eastern Texts and Studies 10. Lewiston, NY: Edwin Mellen.

Stuart, Douglas
- 1987 *Hosea-Jonah*. WBC 31. Waco, TX: Word.

Wolff, Hans W.
- 1964 "Der Aufruf zur Volksklage." *ZAW* 76:48–56.
- 1975 "The Kerygma of the Deuteronomic Historical Work." Pp. 83–100 in *The Vitality of Old Testament Traditions*. Ed. H. W. Wolff and W. Brueggemann. Atlanta: John Knox.
- 1977 *Joel and Amos*. Hermeneia. Philadelphia: Fortress.

HONOR AND SHAME IN THE DAVID NARRATIVES

Gary Stansell

ABSTRACT

This essay examines the David Narratives in 1 and 2 Samuel in terms of the cultural values of honor and shame of the Mediterranean world. With the help of the work of cultural anthropologists, it seeks to demonstrate how honor and shame are significant in the narratives about David's rise to power, his court, family, and political life. David, at the outset of his political career a man of no honor or prestige, seeks and gains repute on his way to the position of highest honor in Israel. But the road David follows is replete with entanglements and relationships of honor and shame with, for example, Jonathan, Nabal, Abigail, Michal, his children, and his military forces. Many elements within the various episodes reflect the social world of the Mediterranean in relation to honor/shame values: the challenge-response pattern, revenge for insults, mediation between disputing parties, family solidarity, and the honor of the male bound up in the sexual purity of the female.

I

The significance of "honor and shame" for the anthropology of the Old Testament is in need of further study and assessment.* Little attention has been paid to this theme by Old Testament scholars since the work of the Semitic philologist Johannes Pedersen, who devoted a chapter to it in his 1926 publication *Israel. Its Life and Culture I-II*.[1] To be sure, "shame" has been the object of investigation in several recent studies, but without particular reference to the notion of honor (Klopfenstein 1972; Seebass 1975; Stolz 1981; Huber 1983; Gamberoni 1986; Kutsch 1986); nor do we lack word studies of the term "honor" (Westermann 1971). In the meantime, however, cultural anthropologists interested in the Mediterranean world have shown a lively interest in, and written widely about, honor

---

*In Memoriam my esteemed *Doktorvater* and friend, Prof. D. Dr. Hans Walter Wolff, D.D.; DDhc. I wish to thank Dr. K. C. Hanson for a careful reading and helpful critique of this essay, which appeared in a different version in *Was ist der Mensch . . . ? Anthropologische Beiträge zum Alten Testament*. Ed. F. Crüsemann, C. Hardmeier, R. Kessler. Munich: Chr. Kaiser, 1992.

[1] Pedersen (1926:213–44) connects honor with the "soul" and its blessings.
For a critique of Pedersen, see among others Hahn (1966:68–74) and Kraus (1969:402–8).

and shame.[2] Their work is beginning to be profitably appropriated for understanding the biblical world. For example, Charles Muenchow interprets Job 42:6 in terms of honor and shame; Bruce Malina presents in detail the case that "honor and shame are pivotal values in the social world of the New Testament and the Bible as a whole" (1981:51).[3] The present essay is concerned with a re-examination of honor and shame in relation to ancient Israelite understandings of what it means to be human. How are human beings pictured in terms of their honor and their shame? Who is honored/shamed, and by whom? In what contexts? What constitutes honor/shame for the biblical person? Furthermore, how might the work of the cultural anthropologist contribute to our understanding of biblical conceptions of honor and shame? For a provisional answer to these and similar questions, the limits of this essay require that we look at a manageable and circumscribed set of texts. Hence in what follows we shall limit ourselves to an examination of the "David narratives" contained in 1 Samuel 16–1 Kings 2. This will provide as a textual basis a cohesive, relatively self-contained set of narratives[4] which exhibits, as I hope to demonstrate, a substantial interest in honor and shame. Moreover, the episodes in the life of David and his court offer a wide variety of themes and settings within which to study honor and shame.

II

The history of David is divided into two sections by many modern critics: 1 Sam 16:14 - 2 Sam 5:10, the History of David's Rise (HDR); 2 Sam 9–20 and 1 Kgs 1 and 2, the "Succession Narrative" (SN); there is some dispute about where the HDR ends and the SN begins. The narratives of David's Rise (HDR) introduce David to the reader by means of three connected but originally independent episodes: David's secret anointing by Samuel (1 Sam 16:1–13), David's appointment as court musician and armour bearer (16:14–23), and David's heroic triumph over Goliath (17:1–58). Among other functions, these stories show how David moves from an insignificant, unknown position—he is a mere youth from the prov-

---

[2] The literature is extensive; the following are some of the more important and are relevant to the subject of this essay: Campbell (1964); especially the six important essays in Peristiany (1966b); Schneider; Berger; Patai; Pitt-Rivers (1977); Herzfeldt; Blok; Wikan; Abu-Lughod, with extensive bibliography; Gilmore; Ginat; Peristiany and Pitt-Rivers.

[3] See also the excellent summary definition of honor in the Mediterranean world of NT times in Malina and Neyrey: 25–46.

[4] On the usefulness of exploring Old Testament narratives in connection with the anthropology of the Old Testament, cf. Childs (1986:198): "...the narrative with its potential for polyvalence is a major vehicle for probing the Old Testament's understanding of being human."

inces—to one of relative status and prospect. After such an introduction, chap. 18 focuses on David's success and Saul's jealous and murderous response to David. Saul, whom chap. 18 describes as "very angry" and "displeased" (v. 8), contrives to bring about David's death. Hoping that David, as his son-in-law, will valiantly fight against the Philistines and be killed, Saul proposes that David marry one of his daughters. First Merab is offered to David; however, she is then given to another man (vv. 17–19).[5] Then, knowing of Michal's love for David, Saul proposes, through his retainers, that David marry Michal (vv. 20–22). It is David's response to Saul's offer, spoken to Saul's men, that is of particular significance for our study.

1. DAVID—A MAN OF HONOR? (1 SAM 18:23)

And David said: "Is it lightly esteemed (הַנְקַלָּה) in your eyes to become the king's son-in-law? And I am a poor man (רָשׁ) and have no honor (וְנִקְלֶה). (v. 23b)

David's reply is often interpreted as a polite answer, expressive of oriental etiquette, not unlike other invitations that must at first be politely refused (e.g., Judg 6:15; 1 Sam 9:21; 2 Sam 7:18; cf. Hertzberg; Ackroyd 1971). While some think David is being properly diplomatic (Alter: 119),[6] lest he seem ambitious (McCarter 1980a:499–500),[7] others take his answer to be merely a humble statement of his economic resources: he is unable to pay the indirect dowry (מֹהַר) (Hanson: 14–15) for a princess (Klein; McKane). But when placed in the context of our question concerning honor and shame, David's words take on a new meaning and significance.

Let us first note the word-play הַנְקַלָּה וְנִקְלֶה, words derived from the roots קלה – קלל II, parallel forms. The basic meaning of the Hebrew קלל is "to be slight, trifling," and in the niphal, "lightly esteemed"; קלה

---

[5] 1 Sam 18:17–19 is not found in LXX^B; some conclude that these verses, including others also omitted in Codex Vaticanus (in chap. 18, vv. 1–6α, 10–11, 17–19, 29b–30), represent an alternative account not originally present in the primitive version of 1 Sam; cf. McCarter (1980b); according to Stoebe (1973), the Merab episode was not an originally independent tradition, but secondary, and cannot be harmonized with vv. 20–30. Perhaps it originally followed 17:25 (cf. Smith 1912).

[6] To the question: what does David feel, or think, as he responds to Saul or his spokesman, Alter stresses that the narrator leaves various readings open in order to suggest David's "fluctuating or multiple motives" as a "political animal."

[7] McCarter argues that David's words, as a protest of unworthiness, are part of an "apology" aimed at showing that David did not "seek to advance himself at court at Saul's expense."

(niph.) means "to be lightly esteemed, dishonoured."[8] With the term נקלה, the verse clearly belongs in the realm of honor and shame language. Indeed נקלה can stand antithetically to the root כבד[9] ("to be honored") and thus may be properly translated in v. 23b with "no honor" (cf. LXX= οὐχὶ ἔνδοξος). The repetition of the word נקלה lends emphasis to David's reply to Saul's men. The first sentence, a rhetorical question (noun clause), apparently expresses David's own sense of the gravity and solemnity of the invitation: this is "no small matter" (*Tanakh*). Connected by a *waw*, the second sentence (also a noun clause) makes an emphatic first-person declaration: *I am a poor man and without honor*. Verse 23b, although similar to v. 18, ought not to be be form-critically understood as a "self-abasement formula."[10] Rather, David gives a presumably accurate assessment of his "honor-rating." Offered the hand of the king's daughter, he responds with a statement about his status and repute; even though he is now a "commander of thousands" (v. 13), he stands before the king's men as a former shepherd who, especially in comparison with the royal family, is an insignificant person, of low status, with no wealth[11]; he therefore is a man of "no honor" (נקלה). Such a first-person assessment of one's prestige and reputation in such a context is a singular statement in the Old Testament.

David's low estimation of his own honor and prestige, when viewed within its context in chap. 18, takes on an ironic sense. For chap. 18, from beginning to end, presents graphic ways in which the formerly unknown shepherd-boy is now gaining reputation and honor. Jonathan gives David his (royal?) robe, his armor, sword, etc. (v. 4)—gestures and symbols that enhance David's status, if not his claim to the throne. The women sing about the mighty feats of Saul and David as they return from battle, and thus honor David equally, if not above, Saul (v. 7). And Saul himself honors David by the invitation to marry his daughter(s) and become his son-in-law. As though to guarantee that the reader not miss the point of all this, the chapter concludes in v. 30 with a summarizing note וייקר שמו מאד; literally, "his name was greatly valued," but Klein's translation more appropriately catches the sense of the phrase within its

---

[8] BDB. Cf. Klopfenstein (184–88); Keller (641–47).

[9] Isa 3:5; Prov 12:9; 2 Sam 6:21–22 (see below, section 4, "David and Michal"); further, כבד//קלל in 1 Sam 2:30; Isa 8:23; 23:9; כבוד//קלון in Isa 22:18; Hab 2:16 (also קיקלון//כבוד); Prov 3:35; 13:18.

[10] Polzin (178), considers v. 23, like v. 18, to be clearly a matter of form, i.e., convention, and applies Coats' (14–26) form-critical designation "self-abasement formula."

[11] Cf. Prov 13:18, which links poverty and dishonour ריש וקלון and places them in antithesis to honor יכבד. The thematic connections of 1 Sam 18:23 with the Song of Hannah in 1 Sam 2 and with the Nathan parable in 2 Sam 12:1–6 should be noted.

context in chap. 18: "and his name was very *honored*." Later in the narrative this verse is picked up by 2 Sam 8:13, where the narrator, in the context of a war-report, says, "And David won a name for himself," i.e., he gained honor and fame.

David's personal assessment of his honor and status in v. 23b, as well as in the whole of chap. 18, stands in instructive contrast with Saul's need for "honor" in chap. 15. There Saul, having been rejected by Yahweh for kingship (v. 26), in a statement acknowledging his sin, pitifully implores Samuel: "Yet honor me now (כַּבְּדֵנִי נָא) before the elders . . . and return with me . . . " (v. 30). Saul's rejection means that he has been dishonored, or shamed. Yet he pleads for a public gesture from Samuel to symbolize an honor he no longer possesses. Saul has lost his honor, and in the future he will be deprived of his kingship. David claims no honor but is soon to be elevated to the throne. Yet, while David himself claims no honor, others will claim it for him.

Indeed, when in a subsequent episode (chap. 22) Saul questions the priest Ahimelech concerning his conspiracy with David against the king, Ahimelech answers, "And who among all your servants is so faithful as David, who is the king's son-in-law. . . and *honored* (ונכבד) in your house?" (22:14). Who, indeed? Ahimelech's defense of David and of himself, disingenuous as it may well be, draws on what must have been court as well as popular sentiment: David has a position of status and honor in the king's house. Thus chap. 18, with its presentation of David's position of honor and his denial of the same, is framed by an earlier episode which speaks of Saul's lost honor (15:26) and by a subsequent one in which Ahimelech ascribes honor to David.[12]

2. JONATHAN'S SHAME (1 SAM 20:30–34)

David's position of honor within Saul's court and his friendship with the king's son lead to the shaming of Jonathan.[13] In chap. 20, David and Jonathan meet to discuss whether Saul's intentions toward David are evil (vv. 1b-3). The issue is to discern the king's intentions (vv. 4–23) and to

---

[12] Ahimelech's words in 22:14 appear to point intentionally back to chap. 18: cf. "son-in-law" חתן in 18:18, 21, 22, 23, 26, 27, used of David only in chaps. 18 and 22; cf. ושׂר ("captain"; presupposed by LXX; MT has וסר; cf. Stoebe 1973) in 22:14 with 18:13, and note the irony in light of 22:2, where, preceding Ahimelech's speech, it says that David was captain (שׂר) over the debtors, the malcontent, etc. David's pre-eminence in faithfulness ("who among all your *servants* [בכל־עבדך] is so faithful") may recall his pre-eminence in success in 18:30b: "David had more success than all the *servants* of Saul" מכל עבדי שׁאול.

[13] On Jonathan as mediator between David and Saul, see Jobling's (4–25) instructive essay.

contrive a way to communicate them to David, who, instead of coming to the feast of the new moon, will hide in the field and await a sign or answer from Jonathan (v. 24). David's absence at the king's table during the festival provokes Saul's suspicious questioning about David (v. 27). Jonathan's answer—that David has gone to a family sacrifice at Bethlehem (v. 29)—causes Saul's outburst of threatening anger, for he apparently sees through the collusion. Saul says to Jonathan:

> You son of a whore,[14] do I not know that you have chosen the son of Jesse to your own shame (לבשתך) and to the shame (ולבשת) of your mother's nakedness? (v. 30)

The verse presents a complex picture of shaming actions within the family: (1) the father, Saul, speaks insulting words to the son, disgracing him (and his mother) in public. Saul's insult to Jonathan's mother here is clarified by what cultural anthropologists know of the Mediterranean area. A woman who has engaged in shameful activity, as Saul suggests of Jonathan's mother, "infects her children with the taint of her dishonour," according to J. K. Campbell (1964:69). Pitt-Rivers concurs: "Honour is a hereditary quality; the shame of the mother is transmitted to the children and a person's lack of it may be attributed to his birth, a consideration that explains the power of *insults* (emphasis mine), the most powerful of all, which relate to the purity of the mother" (1977:29). (2) Jonathan's relationship to David is said to bring shame on him, for he will not succeed to the throne (v. 31). Seebass (53) understands Jonathan to have acted shamefully, not so much because he did an injustice to the king, but because "he had not thought things through carefully and thus had made a fool of himself." (3) Jonathan is also said to have brought shame on his mother('s nakedness). But we may also surmise that (4) Saul himself feels that *he* has been dishonored; for, while Jonathan's friendship with and protection of David obviously has its own political meaning, in terms of honor/shame within the family unit, the son has broken faith with father and family and brought shame on Saul. Thus Saul's shaming of Jonathan is a consequence also of the dishonor Jonathan has brought upon Saul, who is both father and king. Finally (5), the insulting words "you son of a whore" are reinforced by a menacing gesture when Saul casts his spear at

---

[14] Thus translates Stolz; cf. McKane. On the difficult phrase בן־נעות המרדות, literally: "son of a perverse woman of rebelliousness," see McCarter (1980b). Whereas the precise meaning of the phrase perhaps remains unclear (thus Ackroyd), Jonathan, whose mother is called a "rebellious woman," is himself no doubt accused by Saul of being a rebel as well (cf. Hertzberg).

Jonathan (v. 33), a symbolic action that adds to the son's disgrace before the festive table.[15]

The scene reaches its conclusion in v. 34, when Jonathan on the second day of the feast leaves the table in anger, without eating. The reason appears to be given in a double כִּי-clause: "for he was grieved (נעצב) for David, because his father had shamed him"(הכלמו).[16] Some critics think the second כִּי-clause gives the motivation for Jonathan's grief: Saul has shamed *David* (Ackroyd; Klein). However, this is problematic on two grounds. First, Saul has not humiliated David but, more seriously, threatened him with death: he calls David a "son of death" (v. 31 בן־מות); the spear cast at Jonathan, a gesture that is humiliating for *him*, symbolically means death for David (v. 33b). Second, LXX[B] omits the first כִּי-clause. Smith (1912) and others, recently McCarter (1980b), understand the clause, rightly in our view, to be an expansion by LXX. Moreover, in this context, in which David is threatened with death and Jonathan is disgraced, what sense would it make to say that Jonathan "grieves" because David has been humiliated? If the first כִּי-clause is omitted on critical grounds as a secondary expansion, the masculine singular suffix ("him") in הכלמו would then refer not to David but to Jonathan. Hence, v. 34 is not about the shaming of David but of *Jonathan*, whose quick departure from the table is due, not to his "grief" over David's humiliation, but to the insult and humiliation he himself has received from Saul (See Klopfenstein for another perspective on this issue).

This episode suggests that David, who has received public acclaim for his military feats and who has been given a position of honor at the court as hero and as Saul's son-in-law, now, in connection with his intimate friendship with Jonathan, brings (indirectly) not honor but shame upon his friend. The shame is public (at the table of the court); and it is also familial: father shames son (and mother). But the son has also dishonored the father (and the mother) because of David.

3. David Seeks and Gains Honor (1 Sam 25)

The narrative about foolish Nabal and his clever wife, Abigail, who becomes David's wife, exhibits considerable literary artistry, as recent

---

[15] It seems unlikely that Saul intends to kill Jonathan (contra Klein); indeed, Jonathan interprets the gesture as a signal that Saul intends to kill David (v. 33b).

[16] The verb כלם hiph., is usually translated "to put to shame, insult, humiliate" (BDB:484), and can stand parallel to בוש (e.g. Jer 6:15; 14:3; Isa 45:17; 54:4); its noun form can stand opposite כבוד (Ps 4:3).

studies have noted,[17] although 1 Sam 25 hardly presents an original literary unity, as the evident hand of the Deuteronomist indicates.[18] The story has interested its interpreters especially because it exhibits in a didactic manner what a "fool" (נבל) really is; or because it tells how Abigail came to be David's wife; or because it presents Abigail's wisdom and rhetorical skills, which save her neck and enable her to prophesy David's future kingship (vv. 28, 30). But within and behind the narrative, the values of honor and shame also play a considerable role.

David, who has already gathered about him a band of distressed and malcontented men (22:2), is presented as residing in the "wilderness of Maon" (v. 1, LXX; cf. MT פרן), where his men "offer protection" to the shepherds of the rich man of Carmel, one Nabal. David seeks recognition of his services by sending ten of his young men to Nabal during the time of sheep-shearing. David's good wishes ("Peace be to you," v. 6) and humility ("[we are] your servants"; "your son, David," v. 8) hardly mask the threat implicit in the words conveyed to Nabal: "Now your shepherds have been with us, and we did not *shame* them (הכלמנום), and they missed nothing during the time they were in Carmel" (v. 7b). For David to raid Nabal's flocks would have brought dishonor to the wealthy man, likely a clan chieftain of the Calebites[19]; but David and his men have also protected Nabal's shepherds (LXX: "like a wall," v. 30) from other marauders. Now David seeks to be recompensed (v. 8) by Nabal for his "good deeds," which, consonant with an agonistic society, is taken as a "challenge" by Nabal; to pay David for protection brings honor to David and shame to Nabal.[20] Such a challenge requires a response from Nabal, which could take the form of a negative refusal (no response), acceptance, or a positive rejection; choosing the latter, he responds with an insult, employing a defensive strategy which keeps him free of entanglements and obligations. The insult has three parts: (1) a double rhetorical question which derides David by suggesting that he is rootless and his family unknown and without repute (v. 10aβ); (2) a declarative statement which regards David as a rebel, a run-away slave (v. 10b); (3) a further rhetorical question which suggests the foolishness of giving provisions intended for Nabal's servants to persons from places unknown (v. 11; v. 11bβ, "I know

---

[17] Cf. the brief comments in Hertzberg; Stoebe ; also the detailed study by Levenson (220–42); Polzin (205–15).

[18] Cf. Veijola (47–55), who assigns vv. 21–22, 23b, 24b-26, 28–34, 39a (from ויאמר) to the Deuteronomist; see also McCarter (1980b); Klein.

[19] On Nabal as a clan chieftain, cf. Levenson (240–41). Concerning "Calebite," *Qere* is usually read; cf. Targ., Vulg. and Klein.

[20] On protection in connection with honor and shame in Mediterranean society, see especially Pitt-Rivers (1977:34): "To receive protection from someone not recognized as a superior is humiliating. . . ."; also Patai (1976:90).

not where from," reinforces v. 10aβ). That Nabal has shamed David rather than honored him is emphasized later in the story when David blesses Yahweh for holding him back from evil: "Blessed be Yahweh who has 'upheld the case' (McCarter 1980b) of my *shame* חרפתי[21] from the hand of Nabal..." (v. 39).

The point of the challenge-response situation is obscured if Nabal's insult to David is seen primarily in terms of Nabal's character[22]; or in relation to his failure to recognize in David the Lord's anointed; or in connection with guilt because of his negligence of hospitality, brotherliness, or gratitude.[23] Nabal may be "guilty" of bad manners, but his "put down" of David should be seen in the context of Mediterranean customs of challenge and response over claims for honor and precedence. Nabal's words of insult provide the grounds for his non-acceptance of David's challenge to honor him with "whatever you have at hand" (v. 8). For while Nabal is rich and "lives like a king," David is rootless, unknown, a rebel "without genealogy."[24] In an honor/shame society, only equals can strive with one another for honor (Pitt-Rivers 1977:33; Malina: 30). Hence Nabal must reject David's claim that he has "protected" Nabal's flocks; he need not take David's challenge seriously, for David hardly seems to be a threat; he can easily be insulted and dismissed. But the reader knows what the narrator and Abigail know: David is the future king, and as such, he can hardly

---

[21] On חרף II, see Kutsch (209–15), who defines the verb as meaning "(verbally) abuse," "scoff." "He who scoffs at another seeks to denigrate the latter in significance, worth, and ability; he makes it clear that he scorns and despises the other" (p. 211). The word belongs in the same semantic field as בוש hiph., כלם hiph., קלה piel, etc. and is an antonym of כבד piel (cf. Prov 14:31a; 17:5a). The noun "designates the disgrace that one party can 'put' on another," or "the reproach that rests on an individual" (p. 213).

[22] To be sure, the narrative does emphasize that Nabal is "churlish and ill-behaved" (RSV; v. 3 Heb: קשה ורע מעללים); twice he is called "ill-natured" (v. 17 בן־בליעל; v. 25 איש הבליעל), once by his young men and once by his wife, Abigail. בליעל "denotes reprobate, dissolute, or uncouth persons"; its proper meaning is "worthless, useless," according to Gaster (377); perhaps here the narrator has in mind not only Nabal's folly but his asocial behavior; cf. Otzen (1975:135). On the meaning of Nabal's name, see Levenson (221–22).

[23] Abigail speaks of Nabal's "guilt" (v. 24 עון). Stoebe, noting that Nabal's guilt is difficult to pin down, thinks it could be related to his lack of hospitality, brotherliness, or gratitude.

[24] In Mediterranean society "absence of genealogy implies lesser moral worth" and therefore lack of honor; cf. Abu-Lughod (87). If David's family roots are unknown, David is a stranger who in Nabal's eyes deserves only a hostile response; cf. J. K. Campbell (1966:142), who notes that in Mediterranean cultures, hostility between unrelated persons or strangers is "chiefly expressed in aggressive denigration of the reputation of others."

allow a rich shepherd to shame him. Thus he must at least do what a clan chieftain would in a similar situation—seek revenge.

David's decision to take revenge follows immediately upon the report to him of Nabal's words (vv. 12–13; cf. the reaction opposite to David's in 2 Sam. 16:5–14, where David refuses to answer Shimei's insults). In an honor/shame culture, David must respond to the insult; otherwise, he is a coward,[25] and becomes dishonored (Cf. Patai and especially J. R. Campbell 1966:149). "The ultimate vindication of honour lies in physical violence" (Pitt-Rivers 1977:8) and so the narrative continues: "And David said to his men, 'Every man gird on his sword' " (v. 13). But it is not to be, for Abigail intervenes. In the context of challenge and response, Abigail serves as *mediator* between the disputing parties. In Mediterranean culture, the office of mediator is a position of prestige, and thus Abigail accrues honor to herself, even if she is self-selected (Bourdieu: 186–87; Ginat: 60–89). Her mediatorship comprises several elements. First, Abigail takes upon herself Nabal's guilt (v. 24) and then makes excuses for his shabby behaviour (v. 25). Second, she responds to David's challenge by preparing (v. 18) and then presenting gifts (v. 27 הברכה; cf. Gen 33:11) to David. In doing so she acts on Nabal's behalf (but of course without his permission), doing what he refused to do. Nabal dies, not because he has been tricked by his wife (cf. Klein), but because he has been dishonored. Abigail's intentions are of course to spare Nabal from David's vengeance; ironically, her attempts to protect Nabal lead to his death, apparently from a stroke (cf. Wolff 1974a:40–41). Abigail's response to David's challenge acknowledges his honor and thus his superiority. But this act is itself a fresh challenge (or counter-challenge) to which David is obligated to respond.[26] This he does by (1) blessing Abigail and accepting the presents from her hand (vv. 32–35); (2) blessing Yahweh who, by destroying Nabal, has "championed my cause against the insults (חרפתי; see above, note 21) of Nabal" (*Tanakh*) and kept David from evil (v. 39a); and finally, (3) wooing Abigail and taking her as his wife (vv. 39b-40). But the final riposte belongs to the wise woman, who readily accepts his invitation (challenge) to become his wife, an action which brings honor to them both.

The honor/shame aspects of the narrative in 1 Sam 25 have interesting connections with chapter 18. As in chapter 18, David gains a wife. In

---

[25] Pitt-Rivers (1977:5), "To leave an affront unavenged is to leave one's honour in a state of desecration and this is therefore equivalent to cowardice."

[26] Cf. Bourdieu (204), "The gift is a challenge which does honour to one to whom it is addressed... at the same time the gift or the challenge puts to the test the very point of honour that it recognizes in its adversary. Thus it constitutes a provocation and a provocation to reply. The dialogue has been initiated. [One can] choose to prolong the dialogue or break it off." On gifts and honor, see also Pedersen (236).

both chapters, there is bloodshed or death before David can emerge in an honored position (cf. 18:25–27 with 25:13, 26, 31, 39). In both, a marriage is connected with a question of honor and reputation (cf. 18:23, 27 with 25:39). Both stories require the role of mediator (Saul's servants; Abigail). In chapter 18 Saul "honors" David by inviting him to become his son-in-law (vv. 21–23), while in chapter 25 David himself seeks (and attains) honor, in part through a marriage. David's self-assessment of his prestige in chapter 18 ("I am a poor man and have no honor," v. 23) corresponds surprisingly to Nabal's assessment that David is a "nobody," expressed by insulting words about David ("Who is David? Who is the Son of Jesse?" 1 Sam 25:9). But David's self-ascribed position of "no honor" (1 Sam 18:23) is quite different from the same ascription on the lips of another, as the next text in our investigation also makes clear.

4. David and Michal: Double Dishonor (2 Sam 6:16, 20–23)

Michal, introduced in the HDR for the first time in 1 Sam 18:20, is named for the last time in 2 Sam 6:16, 20–23. There, she is the "daughter of Saul [who] loves David"; here, she is the "daughter of Saul (not "wife of David" as in 19:11; cf. 1 Sam 25:43; 2 Sam 3:14) who "despises him (ותבז לו) in her heart" (2 Sam 6:16bβ). The estrangement between the two is clear. The setting of this episode is on the day the ark is brought into Jerusalem in a grand procession and ceremony (vv. 12–15; 17–19). The apparent reason for Michal's contempt is given in v. 16bα, when she "looks out of the window and sees David leaping and cavorting before Yahweh." But as Caird observes, the serious breach between David and Michal "must have had behind it a weightier cause than David's dancing."[27] That the narrator conceives of the estrangement in terms of honor and shame is already implied by the use of the verb בזה.[28] This becomes explicit in vv.

---

[27] Caird; see Alter (123), who notes the multiplicity of meanings possible here: the undignified public spectacle; Michal's jealousy of his glory and her own neglect; David's dynastic ambitions, etc.

[28] בזה ("to despise" BDB: 102) occurs elsewhere within the context of shame terminology, as indicated by Ps 119:22 (חרפה ובוז); Prov 18:3; Neh 3:36 [4:4]; it stands opposite כבד and synonymously parallel with קלל in 1 Sam 2:30. On the word see Görg (1975:60–65). "To despise the king" recalls for the reader the earlier narrative in 1 Sam 10, where "worthless fellows" (בני-בליעל) despise Saul, whom they *dishonor* by "bringing him no present" (v. 27a). The Philistine warrior also "despised" David, because he was but a youth, etc. (1 Sam 17:42). According to the wisdom tradition, it is the unwise person who shows contempt, whether for neighbor (Prov 11:12), within the family (15:20; 23:22), or for instruction (1:7). Thus Michal is a "fool" and, as such, stands in contrast to Abigail, the wise woman. Opposites of בזה are "to be silent" (11:12), "to respect" (13:13) etc.; cf. Görg: 62.

20–22, which elaborate upon and continue v. 16. In v. 20, when David has returned from the ceremony to "bless his household," Michal (again "the daughter of Saul") comes out to meet him. The challenge-response pattern already familiar from the previous text is again found in the ensuing dialogue, which, contrasting sharply in brevity and theme with the dialogue between Abigail and David (1 Sam 25:23–35), reveals biting sarcasm and irony. Calling him "the king of Israel" (cf. the first such instance of the phrase in 2 Sam. 5:3), Michal says:

> How the king of Israel honored (נִכְבַּד) himself today, exposing himself in the sight of his servants' slavegirls, as one of the riffraff[29] might expose himself. (v. 20)

Having despised him in her heart, she now publicly dishonors him by words of reproach. Her claim is not that he danced but that he "flaunted" (McCarter 1984) himself (note the emphasis of the thrice repeated root גלה) and thus made himself appear shameful. That he has done so publicly is underlined by the word לעיני ("in the eyes of" v. 20; cf. v. 22), a word that recalls 1 Sam 18, where "what something looks like 'in the eyes of' everyone in the chapter . . . is revealed to the reader" (Polzin 1989:178; cf. vv. 5 [twice], 8, 20, 23, 26), especially David's honor and success. There David was honored; here, according to Michal, he dishonors himself. But how, precisely? Is it because he is scantily clad and Michal, being a modest woman, is embarrassed by crude behavior? Or because David's dance is part of a Canaanite-Jebusite ritual[30] which must be rejected by a conservative Yahwist? Or rather, do Michal's words have behind them a political meaning: the dancing is connected with the ark's entrance into Jerusalem, a symbol that the house of Saul will have no part in the future kingdom,[31] and thus she is contemptuous of the ark? (Carlson 1964:92). In any case, David responds, first by affirming his intention to dance or "play" (וְשִׂחַקְתִּי) before Yahweh (v. 21), and then by picking up the honor/shame language with these words:

---

[29] According to Smith (1912), the הרקים (LXX apparently read הרקדים), are "wild and reckless men from whom . . . decency cannot be expected." But Ackroyd understands the term more in keeping with the context: "the word implies 'men of no status'." They are "idle"; no prestige, no honor. For Michal, the comparison is apt.

[30] Cf. Porter (164); followed by Carlson (94–95). See the convincing refutation of this view in McCarter (1984:183), who, drawing on the work of Miller and Roberts, argues that chap. 6 "belongs to accounts of ceremonies accompanying the introduction of national gods to new royal cities."

[31] A. Campbell (163). See Brueggemann's (252) lucid discussion which, influenced by the work of Flanagan (361–372), emphasizes the point that kingly legitimacy no longer resides with the house of Saul. The passage's "rhetoric. . . succeeds in driving an irreversible wedge between Yahweh (and David) and the Saulide patrimony now expressed by Michal."

And I will become even more dishonored (וּנְקַלֹּתִי) than this, and I will be of low esteem שָׁפָל in my eyes,³² but in the eyes of the slave girls of whom you spoke, with them I will be honored (אִכָּבֵדָה). (v. 22)

The word ונקלתי, which stands in antithesis to נכבד (v. 21; on the opposition of the terms see below, note 9), recalls David's response to Saul's retainers in 1 Sam. 18:23: ואנכי איש . . . ונקלה. But there he spoke of his relative prestige or honor rating, where the context did not concern actions of David which could earn him censure. Here in v. 22, David responds to the ironic sense of Michal's words: she speaks of his "honor"; he speaks of his dishonor or shame. The phrase translated above as "low esteem (שפל) in my eyes" heightens the sense of the verb ונקלתי.³³ But if David is shamed by Michal and has in her view shamed himself, those of least social status will offer him the honor due a king: "I will be honored" (אכבדה).

Sadly for Michal, the honor due to "the gracious woman" (Prov 11:16) will not be hers. The dialogue having ended, the narrator pronounces dishonor upon Michal in the most devastating manner possible: she remains barren until the day of her death (v. 23). It is beside the point whether this is due to an act of Yahweh or to lack of action by David. Barrenness in ancient Israel and in the surrounding cultures remained a woman's greatest shame—it is חרפה (cf. Gen 30:23). Like Ephraim, her "honor (כבוד) takes flight. No childbirth! No fruitful womb! No conception!" (Hos 9:11).³⁴ Again, we are reminded of the contrast with Abigail, who bore David sons (2 Sam 3:3; 1 Chron 3:1) and thus honored him.

Our passage presents a dialogue or disputation between Michal and David (vv. 20b-22) which is framed by the narrator's report of Michal's feelings (v. 16) and her subsequent (and apparently consequent) barrenness (v. 23): she who has contempt for the king will have no offspring. On

---

³² Thus MT; LXX reads "your eyes"; the point of contrast in the verse seems to be between Michal and the slavegirls, not Michal and David, on which grounds one might prefer the LXX (but cf. Hertzberg: "unerlaubte Erleichterung"). McCarter (1984) and others, e.g., Ackroyd and Crüsemann [1980:224, note 47]), however, prefer "his eyes" (i.e., Yahweh's), following one Ms in MT (BHS),and thus understanding both MT and LXX to contain a scribal alteration for reasons of reverence to the deity.

³³ McCarter (1984), reading "his eyes" (see above, note 45), thinks the phrase refers to David's pious humility before Yahweh, not his shame before Michal. Aside from the textual uncertainty, this does not appear likely, for several reasons: (1) the parallel שפל - ונקלתי suggests parallelism of meaning and would therefore more likely refer to David's *dishonor* rather than *dishonor and pious humility*; (2) v. 22 has moved from a focus on what David does before Yahweh (v. 21) to what David does in the sight of Michal and the slavegirls; (3) the logic of v. 22 is that it of dishonor--low esteem--honor" rather than dishonor--pious humility--honor.

³⁴ Wolff's translation (1974b). Wolff calls attention to the contrast of shame and honor in Hos 9:10–11; Ephraim's "honor," which will be no more, refers not only to a harmonious community life but to "especially the increase of life."

one level the passage is about a familial, even a private matter: the estrangement of husband and wife. On another level, particularly in light of its literary context, it is about a political matter: the break is between king and queen, between the House of David and the House of Saul, which will have no political future. What is important for our purposes is to note that the piece explicitly utilizes the vocabulary of honor and shame to portray both levels of estrangement. In so doing, the passage recalls certain elements in previous episodes in the HDR. On the one hand, it is reminiscent of 1 Sam 20:30–34, where inner familial relationships are spoken of in terms of shame and insult. On the other, its contrasts with 1 Sam 25 are clear. Abigail honors David, while Michal, like Nabal, shames him. And there are consequences: Abigail gets to marry the future king, Nabal dies, and Michal has no children. But, as others have noted, the passage also points forward; David will be even more disgraced in the adultery that is to come (2 Sam 12); yet moments of honor and glory await him as well (2 Sam 12:24; cf. 8:13). And finally, we see again the pattern of the "triangle" apparently required to express human and political interactions of honor and shame: Saul-Jonathan-David; Nabal-Abigail-David; Michal-the slavegirls-David.

5. David and His Men Dishonored (2 Sam 10:1–6a; 19:1–9aba/β)

a. 2 Sam 10:1–6a

The motif of "dishonor for David" is given a different kind of political context within the Succession Narrative in the report of David's Aramean and Ammonite conquests (2 Sam 10:1–11:1; 12:26–31), for which 10:1–6a serves as an introduction.[35] Here David attempts to send condolences to Hanun,[36] whose father, Nahash, king of the Ammonites, has died. Formerly, David had a relationship of חֶסֶד with Nahash, and he intends to continue to "deal loyally" with his son. As we have seen, in an agonistic society, any move to enter into contact with outsiders is perceived as a challenge. The response to David's challenge is met in two ways. The first is the advice given to Hanun by the "princes of the Ammonites," whose

---

[35] Rost (60–62) understands 10:1–6a to be of a different style from what follows in vv. 6b-14, although the former is necessary as an introduction to the latter, giving the reason for the war. 10:1–6a replaces, he suggests, an original, briefer introduction, and was written by the author of SN.

[36] The approach to Hanun, made by David's men, is reminiscent of 1 Sam 25; both there and in 2 Sam 10:1–6a, a challenge made by David's men requires a response; in both the challenge has an element of ambiguity (is it for good or evil?); in both the response is a kind of negative refusal (Nabal: verbal; Hanun: symbolic gesture).

instincts are to avoid entanglements with David. In a private consultation with Hanun, they offer him advice in the form of a double rhetorical question which casts doubt on David's motives:

> Is it to honor (הַמְכַבֵּד) your father in your eyes that David sends comfort to you? Has not David sent his servants to you to search the city, to spy it out and to overthrow it? (v. 3)

The second is a public symbolic act in which David's men have their beards (זְקָנָם) shaved[37] and, with their skirts cut in half up to their buttocks, are then sent away (v. 4). Just as the princes interpret for the king the meaning of David's "honoring" (v. 3), now the narrator explains in a כִּי-clause why David sent to meet his men.

> For (כִּי) the men were greatly dishonored (נכלמים מאד). (v. 5)

The shaving of the beard is an assault on their masculinity, for the beard is a symbol of their honor[38]; to cut their garments, thereby exposing their buttocks and genitals, is an equally powerful act of shaming (cf. Isa 20:4) (McCarter 1984).

David is presented as being sensitive to the dishonor his men have experienced, which he of course shares with them as their leader. He has them remain away from Jerusalem until their beards have grown back (v. 5). But the damage has been done, as the end of the introduction indicates in v. 6a: "And the Ammonites saw that they had made a stench (נבאשו) with David." The verb באש ("to stink," BDB, 920) is elsewhere connected with acts that bring dishonor, and here it means as much as "they had acted shamefully" (Ackroyd 1977), as the LXX suggests (κατῃσχύνθησαν). But it is not for David to take revenge and defend his honor; rather, it is the Ammonites who respond to David's challenge by preparing for war (v. 6b-19). Yet, the honor of the Israelites is demonstrated and affirmed when David's men subdued the Ammonites and their helpers, the Syrians (10:15–19).

b. 2 Sam 19:1–9abaβ

The situation just portrayed is somewhat reversed when, years later, not a foreign king but David himself brings dishonor on his troops. After David's men have defeated Absalom and his followers (2 Sam 18), the king grieves deeply over the death of his son (19:1–3, 5 [Eng. 18:33–19:2, 4]). His grief, grossly inappropriate and incongruous from his warriors'

---

37 MT reads "shaved half of (חצי) their beards"; LXX omits "half of."
38 Cf. Stolz; McKane. On the shaving of hair or beard as a sign of shame, cf. Isa 3:17 (on the text, cf. Wildberger); 7:20; Jer. 7:29, and Pedersen (241).

point of view, is one cause of their shame; the absence of an anticipated rejoicing and congratulations to honor them is another. The depth of their dishonor is emphasized in the passage by the two-fold reference to their shame. First, the narrator reports that the "people stole into the city that day as people steal in who are shamed (הנכלמים) when they flee in battle" (v. 4[3]). Then David, who has "covered his face" (לאט את־פניו) in lamentation over Absalom (v. 5[4])), is rather harshly rebuked by Joab, who says, "Today you have covered with shame the faces (את־פני הבשת) of all your servants" (v. 6[5]). Joab's further words to David elucidate precisely how David's men are dishonored, for David "loves those who hate him and hates those who love him" (v. 7[6]).[39] A following כי־clause both interprets this incongruity and provides an enlightening interpretation of what it means to shame another person: David has acted as if his commanders and servants are "nothing to you" (אין לך). He neither praises nor honors; he is totally oblivious: they do not exist for David. Grief at the death of a son takes precedence over the honor due his troops for their victory.[40] What a contrast with the solicitous David of 2 Sam 10:5, who makes sure that his men remain unseen until their manly honor is again publicly visible. But the circumstances are indeed changed. The potential consequences of the shame David himself has brought on his men is utter desertion (v. 8[7]bβ). The crisis is averted only when David, prompted by Joab,[41] goes and sits in the gate and reviews his troops (v. 9[8]abaβ), an act which we may interpret as giving proper honor and recognition to them, finally, after their victory. But if, as Gunn (1982:103) observes, "David has been deposed," then David himself has been profoundly dishonored by the episode of Absalom's revolt.

6. Shame in the Family: Rape and Incest (2 Sam 13:1–33; 16:20–23)

a. 2 Sam 13:1–33

David's public dishonor is mirrored by the private shame within his family. The story of Tamar's rape, a preface to Absalom's revolt, is told in

---

[39] On love and hate considered as terms of political loyalty, see McCarter (1980b:342).

[40] How is David's grief to be interpreted (cf. Brueggemann 324–25)? His troops are not prepared to be sympathetic. Not only has he failed to honor them; he disgraces himself, and them, by his public show of grief, as analogues from Bedouin culture and the Mediterranean area suggest. Public grief is neither manly nor noble; cf. Abu-Lughod (90).

[41] The triangle of three parties, here David--his troops--Joab, interrelated over a matter of honor/shame, again becomes apparent. Joab, not unlike Abigail in 1 Sam 25, acts as mediator in order to avert disaster.

2 Sam 13:1–33. Amnon, love-sick for his half-sister, Tamar, is aided by the counsel of his friend and cousin, Jonadab, who is "very clever." He constructs a ruse whereby Tamar is brought into Amnon's chamber for the ostensible purpose of "preparing food in his sight" (vv. 5–6). It is, however, not food that Amnon desires, but Tamar herself. Now alone with her, his invitation to sexual intimacy is rebuffed by Tamar:

Do not dishonor me (תְּעַנֵּנִי),
for (כִּי) such a thing is not done in Israel;
do not commit such a sacrilege (הַנְּבָלָה). (v. 12)

The motivation clause (כִּי, v. 12aβ) "refers to serious violations of custom (Gen 20:9; 29:26) that threaten the fabric of society" (McCarter 1984). Such a violation makes Amnon a "fool," or rather, an "outcast," which the narrator emphasizes by the twice-repeated root נבל (vv. 12b-13). The connection between נבלה and actions that shame was already noted in 1 Sam 25; here, however, the term refers not to a "foolish" action but to "sacrilege," a violation of "sacred taboos that define, hedge, and protect the nature of society" (McCarter 1984; cf. also Phillips 1975). Tamar, first attempting to dissuade Amnon from rape ("do not, my brother"), then laments beforehand the shame that will be hers: "But as for me, where would I take my shame?" (חרפתי) (v. 13a).

The deep humiliation of Tamar is stressed by the second occurrence of the root ענה III:[42] "He dishonored her (ויענה) and lay with her" (v. 14bβ), a dishonor compounded by sending her away (v. 16). Tamar's shame is made public when, having been expelled from Amnon's chamber, she signifies her distress by symbolic gesture: "Tamar put ashes on her head, and rent the long robe which she wore; and she laid her hand on her head, and went away, crying aloud as she went" (v. 19). Soon her father, like her, will weep and cover his head in dishonor as he flees Jerusalem (15:30). The outrage must of course be avenged, although her honor thus lost cannot be regained. In Mediterranean society, the sexual purity of mother, wife, daughter, sister is embedded in the honor of the male; accordingly, it is the brother's responsibility to seek revenge in the case of seduction or rape (cf. Pitt-Rivers 1966:42–47; J. K. Campbell 1964:172–73, 200, 271; on Bedouin society, cf. Patai: 120–21).

While the father is angry, Absalom remains silent (vv. 21–22)—until the time is right. The parallels with the story of the rape of Dinah (Gen 34)

---

[42] BDB:776: "to humble a woman by cohabitation." The story emphasizes the "dishonoring" of Tamar by the repetition of ענה (piel) : vv. 12, 13, 14, 22, 32; cf. especially Gen 34:2; also Deut 21:14; 22:24, 29; Judges 19:24; 20:5; Ezek 22:10, 11; Lam 5:11.

are striking. Like Dinah's brothers, who concoct a procedure for slaying not only Shechem but all the males of the city, Absalom has his own plan. He invites Amnon to a festival of sheepshearing (cf. 1 Sam 25:2, 4) which is, in fact, an invitation to his death (13:23–33).

The household of David has been disordered and disrupted. A virgin daughter has been sexually assaulted and shamed. The event has, consonant with the values of an honor/shame society, resulted in death for the one who has destroyed the sexual purity of a virgin princess. But was this also incest?[43] Tamar's words, "Speak to the king, he will not withhold me from you" (v. 13b) suggest the possibility of marriage between brother and sister, at least in the court. But Deuteronomic (27:22) and Priestly law (Lev 18:9, 11) expressly prohibit such a thing. Perhaps these laws were a later development, or not applicable in Jerusalem, as some scholars have suggested. Yet, the "sacrilege" Tamar so emphatically speaks of (vv. 12–13.) suggests that this case is more than rape (cf. McCarter 1984).

b. 2 Sam 16:20–23

If Amnon's rape of Tamar is also to be understood as incest, it is not the last time the royal family is thus to be troubled. Indeed, Absalom, having made political capital out of one incest, is prepared to gain from another. In 2 Sam 16:20–23,[44] a brief episode within the account of the confrontation between Ahithophel and Hushai, Absalom accepts the former's counsel to "go in to his father's concubines" (v. 21). This is typically understood as a symbolic, political act that establishes Absalom's claim to the throne, thus making a complete break with David (cf. Hertzberg; Ackroyd 1977; Stolz 1981, et al.); or, as a "propaganda exercise to show that his rebellion was past the point of return," and thus "he behaves as though he were indeed the king" (Gunn: 138–39, note 4). In the light of Israelite law, which of course forbids sexual contact with the father's wife (Deut 23:1[22:20]; 27:20; Lev 18:8; 20:11), the moral outrage is obvious. Absalom's act also represents a fulfillment of Nathan's prophecy (12:11–12). But there is yet another dimension beside the political and legal. For Absalom utterly *dishonors* his father (he "uncovers his father's nakedness," Lev 18:8; 20:11) by a challenge which, to David's subsequent, profound grief, finds its response in Absalom's death. That Absalom's incest with his father's concubines is understood as a shameful act which causes dishonor is emphasized by Ahithophel's prediction: "For all Israel will hear that you have made yourself stink (נבאשת) with your father" (v. 21bα).

---

[43] For a discussion of incest in the ancient Near East, see Goody (1990:319–25).

[44] These verses have been understood as redactional additions to the original narrative; cf. Anderson.

The word באש, as we noted above in the discussion on 2 Sam 10:6a, can indicate the "committing of a shameful act" which humiliates another person. Indeed, "the fugitive king is put in a position of embarrassment or impotence by the usurper's taking over his rights" (Ackroyd 1977). But like all shame, it is finally public rather than hidden, for Absalom's incest is committed לעיני כל־ישראל, "in the sight of all Israel" (v. 22). The honor of the royal family, which ought to bind its members together and give it repute and prestige, is attacked from within. Brother cannot contain a lust which physically and psychically harms his sister; son cannot bridle his political aggression. Incest and rape become the symbol for the dishonoring of the royal family members: the sister's shame is her loss of sexual purity; acts of shame and violence by the brothers lead to their destruction.

But the honor of the house of David is not extinguished, although its honor appears to be, finally, beyond the grasp of men. Indeed, it can be only conferred by Yahweh. After the David narratives have ended, King Solomon, now successor to his father, is told by Yahweh in response to his prayer (1 Kgs 3:5-9): "I give you also what you have not asked, both riches and honor" (עשר גם־כבוד) (v. 13). And with these words we are returned to David's original self-assessment, "I am a poor man, having no honor" (1 Sam 18:23), the words with which our study began.

III

The honor/shame theme in the David narratives plays a significant role in the way David and those close to him are portrayed. David, at the outset a man of no prestige, seeks and gains repute on his way to the position of highest honor in Israel. While David can be an agent of honor for those who honor him (Abigail), he becomes an indirect cause of shame for others (Jonathan, his men, Michal). Honor and shame within his family are pictured in terms of his estrangement from Michal; of the breakdown of relationships among his children, Amnon, Tamar, and Absalom; and of Absalom's incest with David's wives. Honor and shame in the narratives are thus bound up with friendship, marriage, family life, war—all of course interrelated with the political, under which they are subsumed. Many elements within the various episodes reflect the social world of ancient Israel, as the anthropological studies of Mediterranean societies help clarify: the challenge-response pattern, revenge for insults, mediation, family solidarity, and sexual purity of the female bound up in the honor of the male. While the symbolic gesture appeared as an element in some of the episodes (Abigail's gifts; Saul's spear hurled at Jonathan; shaving of the beard; Tamar's mourning gestures; Absalom's incest), the configuration of a triad, or "triangle" of persons (or persons and a group) was remarkably constant throughout the narratives. This is not unrelated to the public nature of honor and shame, as the repeated phrase "in the eyes of" indicates. Finally, honor and shame in the David narratives as a reflection of ancient Israelite societal values remain, not surprisingly, free of theological reflection and interpretation. It remained for the Chronicler, on the one hand, to enhance David's "honor" by truncating and thus partially suppressing the David-Michal episode (2 Sam 6:16, 20–23), and on the other, to theologize his honor by having David respond in prayer to Yahweh's dynastic promise with the words:

> What more can David say to thee for *honoring* (לְכָבוֹד)[45] thy servant ?
> ... There is none like thee, O Yahweh, and there is no God besides thee ....
> (1 Chron 17:18, 20)

WORKS CONSULTED

Abou-Zeid, Ahmed
    1966   "Honour and Shame among the Bedouins of Egypt." Pp. 245–59 in *Honour and Shame*. Ed J. G. Peristiany. Chicago: The University of Chicago Press.

Abu-Lughod, Lila
    1986   *Veiled Sentiments: Honor and Poetry in a Bedouin Society*. Berkeley: University of California Press.

Ackroyd, Peter
    1971   *The First Book of Samuel*. CBC. Cambridge: Cambridge University Press.
    1977   *The Second Book of Samuel*. CBC. Cambridge: Cambridge University Press.

Alter, Robert
    1981   *The Art of Biblical Narrative*. New York: Basic Books.

Anderson, Albert A.
    1989   *2 Samuel*. WBC 11. Dallas: Word Books.

Baroja, Julio Caro
    1966   "Honour and Shame: A Historical Account of Several Conflicts." Pp. 81–95 in Ed. J. G. Peristiany. Chicago: The University of Chicago Press.

---

[45] LXX presupposes לְכַבֵּד (cf. BHS).

Berger, Peter
　1974　"On the Obsolescence of the Concept of Honor." Pp. 83–96 in *The Homeless Mind*. Eds. Peter Berger, Brigitte Berger, Hansfried Kellner. New York: Vintage Books.

Blok, Anton
　1981　"Rams and Billy-Goats: A Key to the Mediterranean Code of Honour," *Man* 16:427–40; now also pp. 51–70 in *Religion, Power and Protest in Local Communities: the Northern Shore of the Mediterranean*. Ed. Eric R. Wolf. Berlin; New York: Mouton, 1984.

Bourdieu, Pierre
　1966　"The Sentiment of Honour in Kabyle Society." Pp. 193–241 in *Honour and Shame*. Ed. J. G. Peristiany. Chicago: The University of Chicago Press.

Brueggemann, Walter
　1990　*First and Second Samuel*. Louisville:Westminster/John Knox.

Caird, George B.
　1953　"The First and Second Books of Samuel." Pp. 855–1176 in *IB* 2. Nashville: Abingdon.

Campbell, Antony
　1975　*The Ark Narrative*. SBLDS 16. Missoula: Scholars.

Campbell, John K.
　1964　*Honour, Family and Patronage*. Oxford: Clarendon.

　1966　"Honour and the Devil." Pp. 141–70 in *Honour and Shame*. Ed. J. G. Peristiany. Chicago: The University of Chicago Press.

Carlson, Rolf
　1964　*David the Chosen King: a Traditio-historical Approach to the Second Book of Samuel*. Trans. Eric Sharpe and Stanley Rudman. Stockholm: Almquist & Wiksell.

Childs, Brevard
　1979　*Introduction to the Old Testament as Scripture*. Philadelphia: Fortress.

Childs, Brevard
　1986　*Old Testament Theology in a Canonical Context*. Philadelphia: Fortress.

Coats, George
　1970　"Self-abasement and Insult Formulas." *JBL* 89:14–26.

Conroy, Charles
　1978　*Absalom, Absalom! Narrative and Language in 2 Samuel 13– 20*. Rome: Biblical Institute.

Crüsemann, Frank
　1978　*Der Widerstand gegen das Königtum*. WMANT 49. Neukirchen-Vluyn: Neukirchener Verlag.

　1980　"Zwei alttestamentliche Witze." *ZAW* 92:215–26.

Flanagan, J.
1983 "Social Transformation and Ritual in 2 Samuel 6." Pp. 361–372 in *The Word of the Lord Shall Go Forth*. Eds. Carol Meyers and M. O'Connor. Winona Lake: Eisenbrauns.

Gamberoni, J.
1986 "חָפַר II." Pp. 109–11 in *TDOT V*.

Gaster, Theodore H.
1962 "Belial." P. 377 in *IDB* Vol. A-D.

Gilmore, David D., ed.
1987 *Honor and Shame and the Unity of the Mediterranean*. Washington, D.C.: American Anthropological Association.

Ginat, Joseph
1987 *Blood Disputes among Bedouin and Rural Arabs in Israel: Revenge, Mediation, Outcasting and Family Honor*. Pittsburgh: Univeristy of Pittsburgh Press.

Goody, Jack
1990 *The Oriental, the Ancient and the Primitive*. Cambridge: Cambridge University Press.

Görg, M.
1975 "בִּזָה." Pp. 60–65 in *TDOT II*.

Gunn, David M.
1982 *The Story of King David*. JSOT Supplement Series 6. Sheffield: Department of Biblical Studies.

Hahn, Herbert F.
1966 *The Old Testament in Modern Research*. Philadelphia: Fortress.

Hanson, K. C.
1990 "The Herodians and Mediterranean Kinship Part III: Economics." *BTB*:10–21.

Hertzberg, Hans W.
1968 *Die Samuelbücher*. ATD 10. Göttingen: Vandenhoeck & Ruprecht.

Herzfeld, Michael
1980 "Honor and Shame: Problems in the Comparative Analysis of Moral Systems." *Man* 15:339–51.

Huber, L. B.
1983 "The Biblical Experience of Shame/Shaming: The Social Experience of Shame/Shaming in Biblical Israel in Relation to its Use as Religious Metaphor." Dissertation Drew University, University Microfilms International, Ann Arbor, Michigan, no. 1848.

Jobling, David
1978 "Jonathan: A Structural Study in 1 Samuel." Pp. 4–25 in *The Sense of Biblical Narrative*. JSOT Supplement Series 7. Sheffield: Department of Biblical Studies, University of Sheffield.

Keller, Carl
   1976   "קלל." Cols. 641–47 in *Theologisches Handwörterbuch zum Alten Testament II*. Ed. Ernst Jenni. Munich: Chr. Kaiser Verlag.

Klein, Ralph
   1983   *1 Samuel*. WBC 10. Waco: Word Books.

Klopfenstein, Martin
   1972   *Sham und Schande nach dem Alten Testament*. Zürich: Theologischer Verlag.

Kraus, Hans-Joachim
   1969   *Geschichte der historisch-kritischen Erforschung des Alten Testaments*. Neukirchen-Vluyn: Neukirchener Verlag.

Kutsch, Ernst
   1986   "חרף II." Pp. 209–15 in *TDOT V*.

Levenson, Jon
   1982   "I Samuel 25 as Literature and History." Pp. 220–42 in *Literary Interpretations of Biblical Narratives*. Vol. II. Ed. Kenneth R. R. Gros Louis. Nashville: Abingdon.

Malina, Bruce
   1981   *The New Testament World: Insights from Cultural Anthropology*. Atlanta: John Knox.

Malina, Bruce and Jerome Neyrey
   1991   "Honor and Shame in Luke-Acts." Pp. 25–46 in *The Social World of Luke-Acts*. Ed. Jerome Neyrey. Peabody: Hendrickson Publishers.

McCarter, P. Kyle
   1980a   "The Apology of David." *JBL* 99:489–504.
   1980b   *I Samuel*. AB 8. Garden City: Double Day.
   1984   *II Samuel*. AB 9. Garden City: Double Day.

McKane, William
   1963   *1 and 2 Samuel*. Torch Bible Commentaries. London: SCM.

Mettinger, Tryggve
   1976   *King and Messiah*. Coniectanea Biblica, OT Series no. 8. Lund: CWK Gleerup.

Miller, Patrick D. and J. J. M. Roberts
   1977   *The Hand of the Lord: A Reassessment of the "Ark Narrative" in 1 Samuel*. Baltimore: The Johns Hopkins University Press.

Miscall, Peter
   1986   *1 Samuel: A Literary Reading*. Bloomington: Indiana University Press.

Muenchow, Charles
   1989   "Dust and Dirt in Job 42:6." *JBL*:597–611.

Otzen, Benedikt
   1975   "בְּלִיַּעַל." Pp. 131–136 in *TDOT II*.

Patai, Raphael
1976   *The Arab Mind*. New York: Scribners.

Pedersen, Johannes
1926   *Israel: Its Life and Culture I-II*. London: Oxford University Press.

Peristiany, J. G.
1966a   "Honour and Shame in a Cypriot Highland Village." Pp.173–90 in *Honour and Shame*. Ed. J. G. Peristiany. Chicago: The University of Chicago Press.

Peristiany, J. G., ed.
1966b   *Honour and Shame: The Values of Mediterranean Society*. Chicago: The University of Chicago Press.

Peristiany, J. G. and Julian Pitt-Rivers, eds.
1992   *Honor and Grace in Anthropology*. New York: Cambridge University Press.

Phillips, A.
1975   "NEBALAH—A Term for Serious Disorderly and Unruly Conduct." *VT* 15:237–41.

Pitt-Rivers, Julian
1966   "Honour and Social Status." Pp. 21–77 in Ed. J. G. Peristiany. *Honour and Shame*. Chicago: The University of Chicago Press.
1977   *The Fate of Shechem, or the Politics of Sex: Six Essays in the Anthropology of the Mediterranean*. Cambridge: Cambridge University Press.

Plöger, Otto
1981   *Sprüche Salomos*. BKAT 17. Neukirchen-Vluyn: Neukirchener Verlag.

Polzin, Robert
1989   *Samuel and the Deuteronomist*. San Francisco: Harper & Row.

Porter, J. R.
1954   "The Interpretation of 2 Samuel vi and Psalm cxxxii." *JTS* 5:161–73.

Rost, Leonard
1982   *The Succession to the Throne of David*. Trans. M. Rutter and D. Gunn. Sheffield: Almond.

Schneider, Jane
1971   "Of Vigilance and Virgins: Honor and Shame and Access to Resources in Mediterranean Society." *Ethnology* 10:1–24.

Seebass, Horst
1975   "בוש." Pp. 269–72 in *TDOT II*.

Smith, Henry Preserved
1912   *A Critical and Exegetical Commentary on the Books of Samuel*. ICC. Edinburgh: T & T Clark.

Stoebe, Hans Joachim
1973   *Das erste Buch Samuelis*. KAT VIII/1. Gutersloh: Gutersloher Verlagshaus Gerd Mohn.

Stolz, Fritz
    1971   "בוש." Pp. 269–72 in *Theologisches Handwörterbuch zum Alten Testament*. Ed. Ernst Jenni. Munich: Chr. Kaiser Verlag.
    1981   *Das erste und zweite Buch Samuel*. Zürcher Bibelkommentare 9. Zürich: Theologischer Verlag.

Tanakh
    1985   *Tanakh: A New Translation of the Holy Scriptures According to the Traditional Hebrew Text*. Philadelphia: The Jewish Publication Society.

Veijola, Timo
    1975   *Die ewige Dynastie*. Helsinki: Suomalaien Tiedeakamedie.

Westermann, Claus
    1971   "כבוד." Cols. 794–812 in *Theologisches Handwörterbuch zum Alten Testament I*. Ed. Ernst Jenni. Munich: Chr. Kaiser Verlag.

Wikan, Unni
    1984   "Shame and Honor: A Contestable Pair." *Man* 19:635–52.

Wildberger, Hans
    1991   *Isaiah 1–12*. Continental Commentaries. Trans. Thomas H. Trapp. Minneapolis: Fortress.

Wolff, Hans Walter
    1974a   *The Anthropology of the Old Testament*. Trans. Margaret Kohl. Phildelphia: Fortress.
    1974b   *Hosea: A Commentary on the Book of the Prophet Hosea*. Hermeneia. Trans. Gary Stansell. Philadelphia: Fortress.

How Honorable! How Shameful!
A Cultural Analysis of
Matthew's Makarisms and Reproaches

K. C. Hanson

Abstract

The formulaic character of makarisms (or "beatitudes") and reproaches (or "woes") has long been recognized; but often commentators and translators have neglected to take these insights into account. Furthermore, their cultural and theological functions have been largely misconstrued. These forms are part of the word-field and value system of honor and shame, the foundational Mediterranean values; they exemplify the agonistic nature of Mediterranean culture. I propose the translation of "How honorable" for אַשְׁרֵי and μακάριος, and "How shameful" or "Shame on" for הוֹי and οὐαί. Linguistically these translations are confirmed by parallel terms, the antipodal character of makarisms and reproaches, as well as their literary contexts. This affects the interpretation of not only these words, but whole passages (e.g. Ps 112; and Luke 6:20-26). Matt 5:3-10 and 23:13-36 are examined here in light of their linguistic, cultural, and theological importance. Finally the function of these two text-segments is investigated in terms of their location and function within the first Gospel.

INTRODUCTION

One of the most recognizable passages in the New Testament is the opening of the Sermon on the Mount, commonly known as the beatitudes (Matt 5:3-12). These are customarily interpreted as Jesus' authoritative pronouncement of divine blessing on those who embody the listed characteristics. Some scholars have emphasized the eschatological nature of these formulas as promises. English translations, however, obscure the linguistic, and therefore the cultural and theological, distinctions between blessings and makarisms.[1]

Corresponding to the makarisms, the interpretation of the reproaches (or "woes") in Matt 23:13-36 has been similarly misconstrued. Some have

---

[1] This paper was first delivered in Portland, OR, on March 25, 1990, to The Context Group: Project on the Bible in Its Cultural Environment. I would like to thank the members of that group for their suggestions, especially Jerome H. Neyrey, S. Scott Bartchy, John H. Elliott, Bruce J. Malina, and Vernon K. Robbins. David Seeley also offered helpful suggestions.

taken them to be pronouncements of curses or threats, while others treat them as if they were prophecies of judgment or cries of anguish.

In order to understand both the makarisms and woes, however, one must examine them in terms of their relationship to blessings and curses. This is necessary to establish their force as well as distinctiveness. Yet neither makarisms nor reproaches can be properly understood apart from their place in an honor/shame value system, the pivotal values of the Mediterranean. What is required is to demonstrate the traditio-historical connection between these forms in the Old and New Testaments (as well as extra-canonical texts). Furthermore, they all need to be interpreted in their cultural setting in life. These settings have been ignored or poorly interpreted in the past.

I propose, then, to summarize the value-orientation of the ancient Mediterranean. This provides the basis for understanding the perspective of the texts in terms of word meanings and cultural transactions. I will then turn to the force of blessings and curses in order to demonstrate their distinctive usage, followed by a form critical analysis of makarisms and reproaches. Finally, I will address the evangelist's intention in the placement of Matt 5:1–11 and 23:13–36 within the Gospel.

Honor and Shame: The Cultural Sitz Im Leben

Johannes Pedersen first addressed the importance of honor and shame as foundational values in ancient Israelite society. Although criticized for his emphasis on a unique Israelite psychology and linguistic dynamic (Porter; Addinall), Pedersen moved biblical studies forward by recognizing the fundamental role these values played in Israelite society (213–44). But Pedersen's inquiry lacked both a model and a focussed comparative analysis to demonstrate how honor and shame function socially.

Bruce J. Malina's work on the New Testament, building upon recent anthropological studies of Mediterranean societies, provides the analytical model necessary to move beyond Pedersen (1993:28–62; see also Malina and Neyrey 1991). Malina calls honor and shame the "pivotal values" of Mediterranean cultures; and Gilmore refers to "honor-and-shame" as a "master symbol" (1987a:17). That is, they are the values-complex in which all other values are grounded. This conclusion is not based solely upon modern Mediterranean cultures or evidence. It is supported by Semitists (e.g., Pedersen), classicists (e.g., M.I. Finley), Old Testament scholars (e.g., Klopfenstein; Muenchow; Stansell), New Testament scholars (e.g., Corrigan; May; Pilch: 49–70; Plevnik), as well as Mediterraneanists (e.g., Bourdieu; Peristiany; Meeker; Pitt-Rivers 1977; Schneider; Heller).

"Honor" is a positive social value. It is the status which a person claims, in combination with the social group's affirmation of that claim. Conversely, for a person to make a claim of honor and then be rebuffed by the community results in the individual being humiliated, labeled as ridiculous or contemptuous, and treated with appropriate disdain. In other words, honor is not simple self-esteem or pride; it is a status-claim which is affirmed by the community. It is tied to the symbols of power, sexual status, gender, and religion. Consequently, it is a social, rather than a psychological, value.

Speaking of an ancient Greek soldier's honor, Finley observes:

> It is a mistake in our judgement, however, to see the end of the battle as the goal, for victory without honour was unacceptable; there could be no honour without public proclamation, and there could be no publicity without the evidence of a trophy. (119)

In this connection one can compare David's defeat of Goliath. David not only incapacitated the Philistine with a stone (1 Sam 17:49–50), he then stabbed him and cut off his head (17:51). The head is the public manifestation of one's honor, and thus David demonstrated his victory by ultimately shaming his opponent. The head was then taken back to Jerusalem (17:54), as well as brought as a trophy to Saul (17:57). Notice that the vengeance of Herodias (whose honor was publicly challenged) also took the form of having John the Baptist beheaded, and the head was exhibited (Mark 6:14–29; see Jud 13:8–10, 15).

"Shame," on the other hand, may be construed either positively or negatively. Positively, shame is sensitivity towards one's reputation; thus a "shameless person" is one who is not appropriately sensitive, who does not respect social boundaries. Negatively, shame refers to the loss of status: humiliation. The sense is captured in the English "to be ashamed," and "to shame someone," etc.

The assessments of these values move symbolically in opposite directions: Honor assessments thus move from the inside (a person's claim) to the outside (public validation). Shame assessments move from the outside (public denial) to the inside (a person's recognition of the denial) (Malina, 1993:52).

The honor/shame complex is a function of the gender distinctions made in Mediterranean societies. And as the diagrams in Malina (1993:52) and Pitt-Rivers (1966:44) clarify, honor/shame can refer to the ethically defined qualities which everyone in the society upholds (e.g., status, reputation, loyalty). In addition, honor defines the outward qualities in males (e.g., authority, sexual aggression, boldness), symboled in the penis and testicles. This is complemented by shame, which defines the inward qualities in females (e.g., sexual exclusivity, submission, deference), symboled in the hymen (Pitt-Rivers 1966:45; Malina 1981:42–43; Delaney: 40–41).

Mediterranean societies are commonly termed "agonistic"; that is, they are competitive. As the primary value and also social commodity, honor is the object of continuous competition. Each male participates in strategies to maintain his honor and protect the shame of the women in his kin-group. Honor may be either ascribed or acquired. Ascribed honor is the status one has by being born, or by being deputized by a superior; it derives from one's kin-group, gender, order of birth, or delegated authority. Acquired honor is that which one procures through competition, especially in verbal "challenge-riposte" (Malina 1981:30–33; see also Muenchow; and Rowold).

In the verbal challenge-riposte encounters Mediterranean peoples continuously carry on, one may offer either positive or negative challenges. These challenges must be interpreted and then provided with a response. The three phases are thus: challenging action or word (e.g., insult, question, physical blow, or gift), perception (how the recipient interprets the action or word), and reaction (e.g., counter-insult, answer, blow, or reciprocal gift) (see Malina 1981:31; and Bourdieu: 215).

Some narrative examples will make the point. 2 Sam 10:1–19 reports Hanun's negative response to David's positive challenge, all of which is followed by David's negative response in war. John 3:1–12 provides multiple examples of positive and negative challenges between Jesus and Nicodemus. Gal 2:11–14 reports Paul's negative challenge to Cephas' honor, but without noting the latter's response.

The dialogue in Matt 22:15–22, however, provides a classic example of the process. The Pharisees issue what is, on the face of it, a positive challenge; Jesus perceives an attempt to shame him; and he responds negatively to them, and ambiguously to the their question. We can chart the transaction briefly as follows:

> CHALLENGE: "Teacher, we know that you are truthful, and teach God's way truthfully, and defer to no one; for you do not regard people's appearance. Tell us, therefore, what do you think: Is it lawful to pay taxes to Caesar, or not?"
>
> PERCEPTION: But Jesus, aware of their hostility, said:
>
> RESPONSE: "Why put me to the test, you hypocrites? . . . Give to Caesar what is Caesar's, and to God what is God's."

As will be argued below, makarisms constitute a positive challenge, affirming the honor of another, calling for a subsequent positive response. Reproaches constitute a negative challenge to another's honor (viz., public humiliation).

Blessing and Curse

Earlier scholars discerned no difference between formal blessings and makarisms (e.g., Mowinckel, 2:47). While significant work has been done on this topic, it has often been ignored by biblical translators and commentators.

The Hebrew words for blessing are: בְּרָכָה (noun), בָּרַךְ (verb), and the common pronouncement form is בָּרוּךְ (Qal passive participle). The Greek equivalents are: εὐλογία (noun), εὐλογέω (verb); and the common pronouncement form is εὐλογήμενες (perfect passive participle). As both Janzen (1965) and Westermann (1974) have convincingly shown, אַשְׁרֵי and μακάριος may be related to, but are not synonymous with, the terms for blessing.

Blessings and curses are formal pronouncements by someone in authority; in the case of blessing, bestowing God's positive empowerment. This may be from God directly, or from an authorized mediator: usually a king, a priest, or a clan patriarch. Pedersen summarized the fundamental content of blessing as: numerous descendants; fertility of flocks, herds, and fields; and dominance over enemies (Pedersen, 1:204–11). Not only are they formal proclamations, but they are understood as words of power; the words bring the desired result to fruition. Balak, the Moabite king, says to Balaam: ". . . for I know that the one whom you bless is blessed, and the one whom you curse is cursed" (Num 22:6; all translations are my own unless otherwise noted). In hymnic texts, blessing becomes part of the vocabulary of praise (e.g., Ps 145:2).

In Gen 1:28, God directly pronounces a blessing on the primal man and woman: And God blessed them, and said to them: "Be fruitful and reproduce, and fill the land and subjugate it; and have dominion over the fish of the sea, and over the birds of the sky, and over every living thing that moves upon the land." This speech identifies God as the source of blessing. But as a text, it derives from the priestly writers (P), who in all likelihood drew this form from Israelite liturgy.

In 2 Sam 6:18, David is described as pronouncing a blessing at the ritual accompanying the entrance of the ark into Jerusalem for the first time: When David completed the sacrifice of the whole burnt offerings and the peace offerings, he blessed the people in the name of Yahweh of the Armies. David functions here as the mediator of Yahweh's blessing to the congregation at the conclusion of the ritual.

The clearest example of a priestly blessing is the so-called "Aaronic Blessing" in Num 6:22–27:

> And Yahweh spoke to Moses saying: "Speak to Aaron and to his sons saying: 'Thus you shall pronounce the blessing on the community of Israel, saying to them:

> "May Yahweh bless you and guard you.
> May Yahweh cause his face to shine on you and be gracious to you.
> May Yahweh raise his face to you, and establish peace for you."

And they will place my name on the community of Israel, and I will bless them.

This clarifies that the authorized cultic representative (the priest) calls down divine favor on the community so that they may enjoy the benefits of Yahweh's patronage. It also makes explicit that it is Yahweh who bestows these powers of life and protection, not the priest. The priest acts as the mediator of grace; and this takes place in a liturgical setting.

In the Community Rule from Qumran, the priestly blessing of the faithful is coupled with the levitical curse of the wicked:

> And the priests shall pronounce a blessing on all the men who have cast their lot with God—those who walk in integrity in all their ways—and say:
>
> "May he bless you with all goodness,
> and protect you from all evil,
> and illuminate your heart with the insight of life,
> and bestow on you knowledge of eternal matters;
> and may he raise his loyal face toward you for eternal peace."
>
> And the Levites shall pronounce a curse on all the men who have cast their lot with Belial and respond and say:
>
> "Cursed are you in all your wickedly evil deeds.
> May God make you accursed in the hand of all who take vengeance,
>   and assign your descendants to destruction
> at the hand of all who exact reprisals.
> Cursed are you! Hopeless!
> Like the darkness are your deeds.
> Denounced are you into the gloom of perpetual fire.
> May God neither be gracious to you when you cry out,
>   nor forgive for the purification of your sins.
> May he raise his face to wreak vengeance on you.
> And may none of those who possess their patrimony say to you:
> 'Peace'."
>
> And all that enter into the covenant shall respond after the pronouncements of the blessing and curse: "Amen, Amen." (1QS 2:1–10)

This parallels the juxtaposition of blessing and curse in Deut 28:1–24. They are both liturgical, words of power, and pronounced by a cultic leader.

The story of Jacob tricking his father Isaac into blessing him (instead of Esau) provides an example of a patriarchal blessing:

> So [Jacob] came near and kissed [Isaac]; and [Isaac] smelled the odor of his garments, and blessed him, and said: "See, the aroma of my son is like the aroma of a field which Yahweh has blessed! And may God provide for you from the dew of heaven, and from the fatness of the earth, and plenteous

grain and wine. Let peoples serve you, and nations bow down to you. Be a lord over your brothers, and may your mother's sons bow down to you. The one who curses you be accursed, and the one who blesses you be blessed." (Gen 27:27-29)

And in this ancient context, the blessing is not merely a promise, but a formal conferring of favor and an empowerment which cannot be taken back or transferred (see Gen 27:30-40). Like the example from Qumran, this text clarifies that cursing is the reciprocal of blessing.

Westermann contends that cursing did not follow the same tradition history in Israel and was not theologized in the same way: Yahweh does not cast spells or hurl curses (1978:22-23). For the most part, this is true. But the early Israelite community did enact a curse ritual meant to address hidden transgressions (Deut 27:14-26), and Yahweh is the one who curses in Gen 3:14-15 and Deut 28:15-68.

The social settings for these blessings, then, are clearly rituals. On the one hand, God is understood to be the source of blessing. On the other, the three mediators of blessing in ancient Israel (king, priest, and patriarch) indicate the institutional settings of blessings in the two locations of substantive religion in Israel—and the ancient Mediterranean world generally: religion embedded in politics (the king and priest as representatives of national religion), and religion embedded in kinship (the patriarch as head of kin-based religion) (see Malina, 1986). Curses share the attributes of the word of power, and are often employed in the cult setting (see Brichto for a detailed analysis of Hebrew curses).

Makarisms

The term "makarism" in English is a transliteration of the Greek word μακάρισμος. As a technical term it is employed for both Hebrew and Greek formulations. It is often referred to as a "beatitude," stemming from the Latin *beatus*. Gerstenberger calls it a "felicitation" (1988:259). In English translations it is rendered by one of the following (see e.g., Ps 112:1 and Matt 5:3-11 for comparison): "blessed" (KJV, Douay, RSV, NEB, REB [Matt], NASB, NIV); "happy" (JPS, NEB, REB [Pss], NAB, JB, TEV, Dahood: 126); "fortunate" (Allen 1983:93); or "congratulations" (Talbert: 69-72).

I am arguing here that the terminologies of Hebrew אַשְׁרֵי ("honorable") and הוֹי ("shameful"), and their Greek counterparts μακάριος and οὐαι are part of the larger word-field of "honor and shame" (see e.g., Hebrew בָּרוּךְ "honor" and בֹּשֶׁת "shame"; and Greek τιμῇ "honor" and αἰσχύνη "shame"). Thus, of those listed above Talbert's translation is the closest in capturing the sense of honor/shame values.

In most cases the Hebrew אַשְׁרֵי is used in a formulaic expression: אַשְׁרֵי followed by a nominal construction. The three minor variations are: 1) אַשְׁרֵי + noun (singular or plural); 2) אַשְׁרֵי + participle as a substantive (singular or plural); and 3) אַשְׁרֵי + pronominal suffix (singular or plural). The texts which employ these variations are: Singular noun: Isa 56:2; Ps 1:1; 32:2; 33:12; 34:9[8]; 40:5[4]; 84:6[5], 13[12]; 89:16[15]; 94:12; 112:1; 127:5; 144:15a, 15b; 146:5; Job 5:17; Prov 3:13; 8:34; 28:14. Plural noun: 1 Kgs 10:8a, 8b; Isa 30:18; 32:20*; Ps 2:12; Prov 20:7; 2 Chron 9:7a, 7b. Singular participle: Ps 32:1; 41:2[1]; 128:1; 137:8, 9; Dan 12:12. Plural participle: Ps 84:5[4]; 106:3; 119:1, 2. Singular pronominal suffix: Deut 33:29; Qoh 10:17. Plural pronominal suffix: Isa 32:20*. Finite verb: Ps 65:5[4]; Prov 8:32. Relative pronoun: Ps 146:5. Isa 32:20 (*) combines the plural suffix and the plural participle forms, but is listed only once. In four texts אַשְׁרֵי appears as a simple noun (non-formulaic): Ps 128:2[1]; Prov 14:21; 16:20; 29:18. (Numbers in square brackets indicate English versification when different from the Hebrew.)

The formulaic structure of the makarism in the New Testament follows similar lines, but verbal constructions appear more often than in Hebrew. Singular noun: Matt 16:17; 24:46; Luke 11:27*; 12:43; Rom 4:8; Jas 1:12. Plural noun: Matt 5:3; 13:16; Luke 6:20; 10:23; 12:37. Singular participle: Luke 1:45; Rom 14:22; Rev 1:3*; 16:15; Rev 20:6; 22:7. Plural participle: Matt 5:4, 6, 9, 10; Luke 6:21a, 21b; 11:28; Rev 19:9; 22:14. Plural adjective: Matt 5:5, 7, 8; Luke 23:29*; Rev 14:13. Ἐιμί + singular noun (vocative): Matt 16:17. Ἐιμί (subject implied): Matt 5:11; Luke 6:22; 14:14; Acts 20:35. Ἐιμί+ relative pronoun + finite verb: Matt 11:6; Luke 7:23; 14:15; John 13:17; 20:29; Rom 4:7. Ἐιμί + demonstrative pronoun: Luke 12:38; Jas 1:25. Finite verb (subject implied): 1 Pet 3:14; 4:14.

That אַשְׁרֵי and μακάριος are equivalents is established by their one-to-one correspondence in the LXX's translation of the MT. The texts marked with an asterisk (*) combine forms, but they are listed only in the category of their first formulation. In Luke 11:27 one μακάρια modifies two nouns: the first singular ("womb"), the second plural ("breasts"); it is thus a double-duty modifier. Similarly, Luke 23:29 combines a plural adjective formulation and two plural nouns. In Rev 1:3, μακάριος modifies one singular participle and two plural participles. For makarisms in the Apocrypha see: 4 Macc 18:9; Tob 13:14a, 14b; Wisd Sol 3:13–14; Sir 14:1, 2, 20; 25:8, 9; 26:1; 28:19; 31:8; 34:15; 48:11; 50:28; Bar 4:4. For the Dead Sea Scrolls see: 4Q185 1 2.8,13.

For the Pseudepigrapha see: 1 Enoch 58:2; 81:4; 99:10; 103:5; 2 Enoch 42:6–14; 52:1, 3, 5, 7, 9, 11, 13; Joseph and Asenath 16:14 (twice); Pss. Sol. 4:23; 5:16; 6:1; 10:1; 17:44; 18:6; 2 Bar. 10:6; Sib. Or. 3.492, 504, 508, 512;

4.24–26; T. Jac. 2:12–23. For the non-canonical gospels see: Gos. Thom. 7, 19, 49, 54, 58, 68, 69a, 69b, 79a, 79b, 79c, 103; Thom. Cont. 145.1–7.

In addition to these formulaic uses, μακάριος is used in other manners and forms—as a noun μακαρισμός ("honor"): Gal 4:15; ("makarism"): Rom 4:6, 9; an adjective ("honorable"): 4 Macc 7:15; Acts 26:2; 1 Cor 7:40; Titus 2:13; as a divine epithet ("Honorable God/ One"): 1 Tim 1:11; 6:15; and as a verb μακαρίζω ("to honor"): Luke 1:48; Jas 5:11. The two passages in 2 Timothy (both non-formulaic) are the only instances in which μακάριος in any form is attributed to God in the Bible, and are thus closer to the usage one finds in classical Greek.

What do makarisms have in common with blessings? 1) Both makarisms and blessings are affirmative (i.e., positive expressions). And 2) makarisms occasionally extol the same attributes of success as blessings: numerous descendants, fertility, and domination over enemies (e.g., Ps 144:12–15). On the other hand, makarisms are fundamentally different from blessings in a variety of ways. 1) Makarisms are not "words of power." 2) They are not limited to pronouncements by God or cultic mediators. 3) They only refer to humans, and never to God or non-human objects. 4) They do not have their setting in ritual. And 5) one does not pray for a makarism, or refer to oneself with a makarism (see Janzen 1965:223–24).

But if אַשְׁרֵי and μακάριος do not refer to a ritual blessing, neither do they mean "happy." They are not expressions of positive human emotion. One does not feel good who fears Yahweh (Ps 112:1), or walks in Yahweh's law (Ps 119:1), or is reproved and chastened by Yahweh (Job 5:17)! Similarly, one does not feel good who mourns or is persecuted (Matt 5:4, 10). So "happy" is a profoundly misleading translation and interpretation of the makarism (contra Moulton and Milligan: 386, and Louw and Nida 1:302). Even the idea of "imputation of happiness" by others is misleading (contra Janzen 1965:226).

Janzen is similarly misleading in his conclusion when he translates the phrase אַשְׁרֵי הָאִישׁ as: "To be envied is the man . . ." or "Enviable is the situation of the man . . ." (1965:225). Janzen recognizes that the English word "envy" can have positive or negative connotations, and he wants to stress the positive in this formula. What he overlooks is how misleading this translation is in terms of representing a Mediterranean perspective. In the Mediterranean, envy is associated with casting the evil eye, wishing misfortune, and greed (see e.g., Gen 30:1; Deut 15:9; 1 Sam 2:22; Sir 14:3–10; Mark 7:32; and Elliott, 1988, 1990, 1991, 1992).

If makarisms are neither authoritative blessings nor joyous emotions, what are they? Janzen has clearly seen that they are fundamentally affirmations made by an individual or community about someone else. His diagram illuminates the relationship and difference between blessing and makarism:

FIGURE #1: BLESSING AND MAKARISM TRANSACTIONS

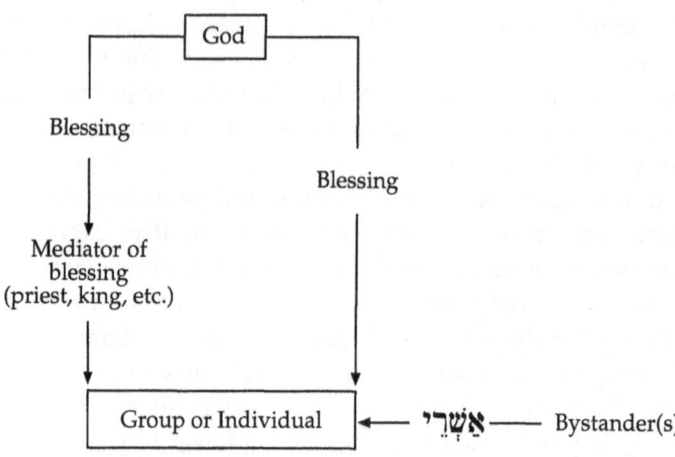

What Janzen has not seen is that these affirmations are exclamations of honor and esteem, understandable only in terms of the Mediterranean competition for honor. In virtually every formulaic instance of אַשְׁרֵי and μακάριος one could translate "How honored" or "O how honorable." In Janzen's diagram it is "bystanders" (better: one's community of orientation) who pronounce makarisms, which demonstrates the basic issue with regard to honor: it is one's self-respect in conjunction with the community's affirmation of that evaluation. As already mentioned, honor moves from personal claim to public validation. Makarisms thus represent the public validation of an individual's or group's experience, behavior, or attitude as honorable.

Linguistically, this translation is confirmed by the terms which parallel it. Ben Sira includes two formal makarisms in his list of ten honorable considerations:

> Nine considerations have I honored (ἐμακάρισα) in my heart, and the tenth I will utter with my tongue . . .
> O how honorable (μακάριος) is the one who lives with an understanding wife . . .
> O how honorable (μακάριος) is the one who has found prudence . . . (Sir 25:7, 8, 9).

The precise meaning of μακάριος is clear in the parallel construction. It is juxtaposed to two other expressions, and they all express honor and praise: "O how great" (ὡς μέγας; 25:10a) and "but no one exceeds" (ἀλλ' οὐκ ἔστιν ὑπέρ; 25:10b). Antithetically, whenever אֶשֶׁר and μακάριος are paralleled, it is virtually always by אוֹי / הוֹי and οὐαι (see the evidence below).

This is further confirmed by the adjectives parallel to μακαρίου in 4 Macc 7:15:

> O one of honorable age (μακαρίου γήρως),
> and of venerable (σεμνῆς) gray hair,
> and of law-abiding (νομίμου) life,
> whom the faithful seal of death has perfected.

Here, Eleazar's age is not "happy" or "blessed," but honorable. He is deserving of honor because of being an elder in the community, as well as committed to the law.

In 2 Kings 10, the Queen of Sheba demonstrates this public validation by acknowledging the benefits which Solomon's household derived from his presence. The honor of Solomon is reflected in the advantage and prestige which those around him share: "O how honored are your wives! O how honored are your servants, who continually stand before you and listen to your wisdom!" (1 Kgs 10:8; par. 2 Chron 9:7; see Luke 11:27). As Westermann rightly concludes, this text demonstrates that the original setting of the Hebrew makarism is in direct address: well-wishing or congratulations at a meeting or everyday encounter, which would entail a second person formulation (1974:192, 195). But he also notes that second person formulations are rare (see Ps 128:3[2]; Isa 30:20). Notice how the makarism has maintained its second person character in the Hellenistic Greek formulation: "O honorable one!" (ὦ μακάριε; Josephus, Ant. 19.1.13 [97]). Another example of the second person formulation is Matt 16:17: "How honorable are you, Simon Bar-Jonah; for flesh and blood has not revealed this to you, but my Father in heaven." Compare also Matt 13:16 (par. Luke 10:23); Luke 1:42a, 42b; and Iliad 1.182.

Westermann (1974:191–95) goes on to distinguish three usages of the makarism in the Old Testament: 1) congratulations for success (e.g., 1 Kgs 10:8; Deut 33:29); 2) congratulations for behavior (e.g., Ps 1:1; Prov 14:21); and a usage which stands between the other two: 3) congratulations for those who trust in God (e.g., Ps 40:5; Isa 30:18). Westermann's breakdown is marginally helpful in perceiving different emphases. This clouds, however, the fundamental unity of these formulations. Each of them is a *value judgment* made by an individual, or the community at large, on either a real or an ideal person. It is the social imputation of esteem to an individual or group for manifesting desirable behavior and commitments.

The same argument can be made against Betz's categories: cultic, secular, ethical-paraenetic, apocalyptic, and "makarisms of the wise man" (30–34). These classifications really speak to different literary contexts or emphases. They do not, however, change the fundamental issue that, whatever their context, all makarisms are formally unified, and they articulate the values of the community, sage, or teacher, and pronounce the subject/s "honorable."

Makarisms came to have a specialized use in third person formulations (singular and plural) to affirm and validate values which the community wishes to hold up as honorable: the ideals of behavior. This is most clearly seen in Ps 112. Here, in an alphabetic acrostic poem, a sage enumerates the attributes of -the ideal Judean male, characterized as: "the man who fears Yahweh" (אִישׁ יָרֵא אֶת־יהוה, v 1), "the good man" (טוֹב אִישׁ, v 5), and "the righteous one" (צַדִּיק, v 6) (see Hanson: 142–84). This constitutes a portrait of honorable behavior and its expected rewards. For example, he delights in Yahweh's commandments (v 1b); he is gracious, merciful, and righteous (v 4b); he is gracious, lends, and executes his actions with justice (v 5, 9a); he is not fearful (v 7). We can summarize all of this by translating v 1: "O how honorable is the man who . . ." This is the sort of person the community affirms because he acts for the benefit of, and in solidarity with, his community. The opening phrase of Ps 112 grounds all of this person's other honorable traits in his theological commitment: his honorable behaviors in the community are rooted in his honorable loyalty to Yahweh.

The third person formulation appears often in the New Testament: e.g., "How honorable is the one who is not scandalized by me" (Matt 11:6; par. Luke 7:23). Like those in the Old Testament, one finds makarisms pronounced upon both specific persons (e.g. Matt 16:17; Luke 1:45) and more generally upon those who uphold the values of the Christian community (e.g., Rom 14:22; Rev 1:3). The connection to values is made especially clear in the fact that makarisms often occur in series: e.g. Ps 32:1–2 (par. Rom 4:7–8); Matt 5:3–10, 11; Luke 6:20–22; Rev 1:3a, 3b; Sir 14:1–2; 25:8–9; 2 Enoch 42:6–14; 52:1–14; Gos. Thom. 79a-c; Thom. Cont. 145.1–7.

Luke 11:27–28 provides an interesting juxtaposition of a third person singular makarism (referring to Jesus' mother), countered by a third person plural makarism (spoken by Jesus): "And it happened as he said this, a certain woman called out from the crowd: 'O how honorable (μακάριος) is the womb who bore you, and the breasts you sucked!' But he said: 'Rather—O how honorable (μακάριος) are the ones who hear God's word and keep it!'" (compare John 13:17). The woman's makarism, while in third person form, retains the personal and dialogical character of honoring (positive challenge), as already seen in 1 Kgs 10:8. Their juxtaposition, then, emphasizes the shift of esteem from the particular (Jesus' mother) to the general (all who obey God's word). One could also read this as Jesus' positive response to a positive challenge: she honors him and his mother, and he in turn honors all those responsive to God's word.

An example of how the Greek use of μακάριος fits in with honor/shame and community ideals is found in Josephus's account and explanation of Judah Maccabee's speech to his troops before battle. Here he positively challenges their honor (although μακάριος is used as a simple adjective):

> Since, therefore, at the moment it lies in your power either to recover this liberty and regain a prosperous (εὐδαίμονα) and honorable (μακάριον) life—by this he meant one in accordance with the laws and ancestral customs—"or to endure the shame (αἴσχιστα), and to leave your people without descendants by being cowardly in battle. You yourselves must fight, then, since those who do not fight will also die; believing that suffering for such great causes—freedom, patrimony, laws, worship—secures you perpetual honor (εὔκλειαν)." (Ant. 12.7.3 [303–304])

He argues that the prosperous and honorable life is the one which accords with law and custom, exemplifies courage in battle, and endures suffering on behalf of the community. The recompense for that sort of life, Judah contends, is a reputation perpetually honored by the community. He calls to their attention that to do otherwise is to open themselves up to shame. This is the epitome of an honor/shame transaction.

Two non-biblical examples of makarisms further illustrate the emphasis on honor and relative status. The first is found in Josephus, where the Queen Mother is discussing the succession to the throne of Adiabene and pronounces a "political" makarism: "How honored (μακάριος) is the one who, not from one, but from the many, receives authority" (Ant. 20.2.2 [24]). Another example is from the Sentences of Sextus (second century CE): "How honorable (μακάριος) is the man whose soul is not detained journeying toward God" (Sentence #40).

To interpret the makarisms in terms of honor provides an explanation for Janzen's observation that neither Yahweh nor non-human objects are ever the subject of a makarism (1965:225–26): only humans play the challenge-riposte "game" of honor. One may also explain Westermann's observation that the third person formulations seem to have eclipsed the second person formulations: אַשְׁרֵי and μακάριος primarily came to characterize socially ideal behavior and commitments.

Reproach

The term "reproach" (German: *Scheltwort*) was used by early form critics to refer to the reasons for a divine judgment: e.g., Isa 1:2–3; Jer 2:10–13 (Gunkel: 74). This was dropped by later form critics, who demonstrated that the term was misleading: what was really being described was an "accusation" (Wolff, 1934; Westermann, 1967:64–70). I follow Scott in his identification of the woe-formula as a reproach and his translation of הוֹי as "Shame!" or "Shame on" (179–80). But this should not be interpreted lightly, as it would be taken in English. Rather, in Mediterranean societies this is understood as a serious challenge to the honor of those addressed. To be shamed means the loss of status, respect, and worth in the community.

English-speaking scholars have traditionally called reproaches "woe-oracles" (see e.g., Whedbee: 80–110; Janzen 1972). The problem with this is that these sayings are rarely reported as part of a Yahweh speech, and they are thus not generically "oracles" (see Tucker: 340)—a problematic term in any case. At least the term "woe cry" (German: *Weheruf* or *Wehe-Worte*) used by Westermann (1967:190) and Wolff (1973:17–34; 1977:242–45) is a relatively neutral formulation. Some have persisted in interpreting the reproaches in terms of funeral lamentations even within the prophetic sayings (e.g., Clifford: 464; Holliday: 594). These translations/interpretations ignore the cultural meaning of the term. The full import of "shame" must be kept in view through an understanding of the cultural meaning and its Sitz im Leben.

While it retains the unfortunate term "woe oracle," the most concise definition of this speech form appears in the glossary of *The Forms of the Old Testament Literature*:

> A genre that is used in the prophetic literature to criticize particular actions or attitudes of people, and sometimes to announce punishment upon them. Woe oracles are found as individual units (Isa 1:4; 3:11; 10:5) or in a series (Isa 5:8–24).
> The typical woe oracle has two parts: (1) the exclamation הוֹי ("woe") followed by a participle denoting the criticized action, or a noun characterizing people in a negative way, and (2) a continuation with as variety of forms, including threats (Isa 5:9, 13–14, 24; 28:2–8), accusations (Ezek 13:3–9; 18:19 [sic: 13:18, 19]), or rhetorical questions (Isa 10:3–4; Amos 6:2). This genre was likely adopted by the prophets from wisdom circles (Gerstenberger, Wolff, Whedbee). (Hals: 358–59)

The basic reproach formula is thus: הוֹי + a nominal construction. There are several variations. Singular proper noun: Isa 10:5; 29:1; Jer 48:1. Singular common noun: Isa 1:4; 18:1; 28:1; Jer 23:1; Nah 3:1; Zech 11:17. Plural common noun: Isa 30:1; Ezek 13:3; 34:2. Singular participles: Isa 45:9, 10; Jer 22:13; Hab 2:6, 9, 12, 15, 19; Zeph 3:1. Plural participles: Isa 5:8, 11, 18, 20; 10:1; 29:15; 31:1; Ezek 13:18; Amos 5:18; Mic 2:1; Zeph 2:5. Preposition + singular pronominal suffix: Jer 50:2. Plural adjective: Isa 5:21, 22; Amos 6:1.

Three proposals have been made to account for the *Sitz im Leben* of the reproaches: 1) weakened forms of curse, with their setting in the cult, and variations on the prophetic judgment speech (Westermann 1967:189-98); 2) adaptations from funeral laments (Wright: 32; Clifford; Wanke: 215-18; Janzen 1972); and 3) sages' reflections on worldly conditions (Gerstenberger 1962; Wolff 1973:17-34). For a discussion of these proposals, see Whedbee: 86, 93-98).

Westermann is correct in seeing an overlap between curse and reproach in form (the participial form following the curse or הוֹי) and content (social behavior). The problem is that the reproach is fundamentally different from curse, since the curse (like the blessing) is usually pronounced by an authoritative figure: priest (e.g. Deut 27:14-26), diviner (e.g., Num 22:6), patriarch (Gen 27:39), political leader (Josh 6:26), or divinely commissioned messenger (2 Sam 16:7-8, 10-11).

Gerstenberger's argument rests first on form: it is the polar opposite of אַשְׁרֵי (see e.g., Isa 3:10-11; Qoh 10:16-17; Sir 10:16-17; Luke 6:20-26). Secondly, the contents of the "woe" formulations are the problems of social ethos commonly addressed in the wisdom literature: oppression of the poor (e.g., Isa 10:1-2//Prov 14:31), illegal acquisition of property (Isa 5:8//Prov 23:10), drunkenness (Isa 5:11-12//Prov 23:29-35), etc. (see Whedbee: 86, 93-98). Qoh 10:16-17 is the clearest case of juxtaposing a reproach and a makarism in the setting of community honor and shame:

> Shame (הוֹי) on you, O land,
>   when your king is a client,
>   and your princes feast in the morning.
> How honored (אַשְׁרֵי) are you, O land,
>   when your king is the son of the free,
>   and your princes feast at the appropriate time:
>   for strength, and not for drunkenness!

(The emendation of הוֹי for a nonsensical אִי is supported by the LXX: οὐαί.)

Further confirmation of the antipodal relationship of makarisms and reproaches, however, comes from outside the canon of Scripture. In 1 Enoch 103:5-6 a reproach (which represents the author's viewpoint) contrasts a makarism (which represents the viewpoint of the wicked):

> Shame on you sinners who are dead! When you are dead in the wealth of your sins, those who are like you will say of you, "How honorable are you sinners! The sinners have seen all their days. They have died now in prosperity and wealth...." (modified from Isaac: 84)

In 2 Enoch 52:1-15, one finds an alternating series of seven makarisms and seven reproaches. The only extant manuscripts are in Slavonic (the original was probably Aramaic, Hebrew, or Greek), but their character as makarisms and reproaches is unmistakable. Notice that they also speak of social ethos issues:

> How honorable is the one who opens his lips for praise of the God of
> Sabaoth, and praises the LORD with his whole heart.
> How shameful is everyone who opens his heart for insulting,
> and insults the poor and slanders his neighbor;
> because that one slanders God.
> How honorable is the one who opens his lips,
> both blessing and praising God.
> How shameful is the one who opens his lips for cursing and blasphemy
> before the Lord all his days.
> How honorable—whoever blesses all the works of the LORD.
> How shameful—whoever despises any of the LORD's creatures.
> How honorable—whoever looks carefully to the raising up of the works
> of his own hand.
> How shameful—whoever looks and is jealous to destroy another.
> How honorable—whoever preserves the foundations of his most ancient fa-
> thers, made firm from the beginning.
> How shameful—he who breaks down the institutions of his ancestors and
> fathers.
> How honorable—whoever cultivates the love of peace.
> How shameful—whoever disturbs those who are peaceful by means of love.
> How honorable—whoever, even though he does not speak peace with his
> tongue, nevertheless in his heart there is peace toward all.
> How shameful—whoever with his tongue speaks peace, but in his heart there
> is no peace, but a sword.
>
> (modified from Andersen: 178–81)

Another text which juxtaposes reproaches and makarisms is The Book of Thomas the Contender. Twelve reproaches (143.8–144.40) are juxtaposed to three makarisms (145.1–7):

> Shame on you, O godless people without hope . . . Shame on you who put your hope in the flesh and the prison that will perish . . . Shame on you for the fire that burns within you . . . Shame on you because of the wheel turning in your thoughts. Shame on you who are gripped by the burning that is in you . . . Shame on you who are captives . . . Shame on you who dwell in error . . . Shame on you who love the sexual intercourse that belongs to femininity and its foul cohabitation. Shame on you who are gripped by the authorities of your bodies . . . Shame on you who are gripped by the agencies of wicked demons. Shame on you who beguile your limbs with fire . . . Shame on you, for you have not accepted the teaching . . .
>
> Honored are you who have already understood temptations and have fled from alien things. Honored are you who are mocked and are not honored because of the love your lord has for you. Honored are you who weep and who are caused distress by those who have no hope: for you will be freed from every kind of bondage. (modified from Layton: 407–9)

For other couplings of makarisms and reproaches, see also 1 Enoch 99:10–16; Gos. Thom. 102–103; 2 Bar. 10:6–7; b. Ber. 61b; b. Yoma 87a.

Following the arguments of Gerstenberger, I conclude that the reproach formula or "woe" (הוֹי, οὐαι) is the antithesis and antipode of the makarism formula (אַשְׁרֵי; μακάριος). Parallel to the אַשְׁרֵי formulation, then ("How honorable are those who . . ."), I propose the translation of the reproach ("woe") formula as: "O how shameful are those who ...," "Shame on ...," or "How disreputable are those who ..." A few examples will suffice:

> O how shameful (הוֹי) are those who are at ease in Zion,
> and those who are secure on the Samarian mount.... (Amos 6:1)

> O how shameful (הוֹי) are those who call evil "good," and good "evil";
> who replace darkness for light, and light for darkness;
> who replace bitter for sweet, and sweet for bitter.
> O how shameful (הוֹי) are those wise in their own eyes,
> and discerning in their own view.
> O how shameful (הוֹי) are those mighty at wine drinking
> and prodigious at mixing liquor,
> who pardon the guilty for a bribe,
> and who deprive the innocent of their rights. (Isa 5:20–23)

One might conclude from the number of occurrences that while the reproaches may have originated among the sages, or the ethos of the clan (with Gerstenberger, Wolff, and Whedbee), the prophets no longer employed them as challenges to the honor of the community. But they have indeed retained their character as challenge. This is indicated first by the formal separation of the reproach from appended threats or accusations. That is, the disreputable behaviors articulated in the reproaches are often the basis for the prophetic threats, but not always. Even if a threat follows, the prophets first label the behavior as reprehensible in the form of a reproach, as a challenge to the public honor of the perpetrators. Furthermore, the introduction to the series of reproaches in Hab 2:6–19 identifies the oral character of these reproaches, and that they would be uttered by the community (see also 1 Enoch 103:5–6). Furthermore, this series highlights the honor/shame values at stake, as well as the "challenge-riposte" dynamic:

> Shall all these not take up a taunt (מָשָׁל) against him, in
> scoffing derision (מְלִיצָה חִידוֹת) of him: "Shame (הוֹי) on
> the one who heaps up what does not belong to him,—how
> long?—and loads himself up with pledges!... Shame (הוֹי)
> on the one who accumulates evil gain for his house... You have
> counseled your house shamefully (בֹּשֶׁת)... Shame (הוֹי)
> on the one who builds a city with blood, and establishes a village
> on injustice. Shame on (הוֹי) the one who makes his neighbor drink
> from the cup of his violence, and makes him drunk in order
> to gaze on his genitals. You are satisfied with contempt (קָלוֹן)
> instead of honor (בָּרוּר)... and contempt (קָלוֹן) will
> cover over your honor (בָּרוּר)." (Hab 2:6, 9a, 10a, 12, 15, 16a, 16d)

The prophetic use of the reproach does not change its definition as a negative challenge to honor in the least. Gerstenberger (1962), Wolff (1973), and Whedbee have all demonstrated that the prophets employed the formula in relation to the social ethos, in line with the concerns of the sages. Furthermore, Westermann keenly observed that the classical "introductory messenger formula" (כֹּה אָמַר יהוה, "Thus says Yahweh ...") seldom appears in conjunction with the reproaches. In fact, of the thirty-six occurrences of the reproach formula in the prophets, only three are introduced by the messenger formula: Jer 48:1; Ezek 13:18; 34:2. Three more are employed in reports of Yahweh speeches (Isa 30:1; Jer 23:1; Ezek 13:3). Thus the prophetic use of the reproach in divine speech constitutes a secondary development, and a minor variation. In these few cases it is Yahweh who challenges the honor of the respective groups. And setting the New Testament makarisms in the setting of early Christian prophecy is also thereby weakened. I believe a stronger case can be made for maintaining their setting in didactic wisdom settings, whether from Jesus or the early Christian communities (contra Boring: 26–27).

The Greek οὐαι formula parallels the Hebrew construction; οὐαι is followed by a nominal construction, and sometimes a reason or a threat. The different variations on the formulaic use are as follows. Singular pronoun: 1 Cor 9:16. Plural pronoun: Luke 11:44, 47; Jude 11. Pronoun + singular proper noun: Matt 11:21a, 21b; Luke 10:13a, 13b. Pronoun + plural common noun: Matt 23:13, 15, 16, 23, 25, 27, 29; Luke 11:42, 43, 46, 52. Singular common noun: Matt 18:7a, 7b; Mark 14:21; Luke 17:1b; 22:22; Rev 12:12. Plural participle: Matt 24:19; Mark 13:17; Luke 6:25a; 21:23; Rev 8:13. Plural adjective: Luke 6:24a, 25b. Adverbial clause: Luke 6:26. Besides these formulaic uses, οὐαι also appears as a simple noun (Rev 9:12; 11:14). For reproaches with οὐαι in the Apocrypha see: Jud 16:17; Sir 2:12–14; 41:8. Reproaches with the Latin equivalent (vae) appear in: 2 Esd 2:8; 15:24, 47; 16:1a, 1b, 63, 67. For other ancient Judean and Christian reproaches, see: 4Q184 1.8; 4Q378 6 1.7; 4Q404 10 1.1; 4Q511 63 3.5; 4QapLam 1.10; 6QHymn 1.7; MasShirShabb 1.2; 1 Enoch 94:6–8; 95:4–7; 96:4–8; 97:7–8; 98:9–99:2; 99:11–16; 100:7–9; 103:5; 2 Enoch 52:4, 6, 8, 10, 12, 14; Sib. Or. 2.339–44; 5.89–91; 7.118–19; 8.95–99; Gos. Thom. 102; Pap. Oxyr. 840; Prot. Jas. 3.1b, 2a, 2b, 2c, 3a, 3b; Inf. Thom. 19.4.

In the New Testament the term οὐαι (parallel to the Hebrew הוֹי) is also used in the sense of a funeral cry, "Alas!" (Rev 18:10, 19), in addition to the reproach of "O how shameful," or "Shame on." The unique use in scripture of the reproach against oneself by Paul in 1 Cor 9:16 ("Shame on me if I do not preach the gospel!") identifies how one can shame oneself. The Stoic Epictetus (1st century CE) argues that the difference between a common individual (ἰδιώτος) and a philosopher is that the former thinks his honor can be compromised by his kin, while the latter knows that he can only shame himself:

The first difference between an [ordinary] individual and a philosopher: one says, "Shame on me because of my child, because of my brother; shame because of my father"; the other—if he can be constrained to say "Shame on me," he stops and says, "because of me." (Discourses 3.19.1)

Similarly, Anna pronounces six reproaches upon herself for the shame that she experiences because of her childlessness (Prot. Jas. 3.1–3). After the first, she adds: "And I was reproached, and they mocked me and thrust me out of the temple of the Lord" (3.1c; Cameron: 111). This provides further support for the honor/shame character of the reproaches: Anna's shame derives from her own lack and the corresponding humiliation by her community. Anna's shame is internalized from the initial public humiliation. Compare this to the Sibyl's self-reproach for not caring for the needy (Sib. Or. 2.339–44); this shame is experienced because the behavior is revealed at the judgment.

MATTHEW 5:3–10

My interest here in the makarisms and reproaches in Matthew 5 and 23 is not to address their specific contents or Matthew's sources (for these see e.g.: Strecker 1971; Guelich 1982:63–118; Betz; Lambrecht: 45–73; Luz: 226–44). Rather, I want to address their form, and the function of their placement in the Gospel.

The eight makarisms in Matt 5:3–10 are a unified text-segment, even if this unity is a product of the evangelist's redaction rather than his source or the oral tradition. Matt 5:1–2 provides a redactional introduction to the whole "sermon," paralleling the conclusion in 7:28–29. And the expansive makarism in 5:11–12 appears to have been appended to the series: it is a second person formulation (as opposed the third person forms in vv. 3–10); it employs an εἰμί formulation + a three-part adverbial clause (while substantives appear in vv. 3–10); it emphasizes relationship to Jesus (vv. 3–10 focus on general ethical behavior); it is expanded with a two-fold exhortation + motivation + explanation (as opposed to the simpler makarism + ὅτι clause in vv. 3–10). Nonetheless, in the final form of the Gospel, 5:11–12 must be taken as part of the series of makarisms. Since the position of 5:5 is fluid in the manuscript traditions, and is an adaptation of Ps 37:11a, it may be a late addition to Matthew's original seven (Dodd: 2).

The form of the makarisms is: μακάριος + plural substantive (noun, adjective, or participle) + motivational clause (ὅτι "for" + plural pronoun + verb or verbal phrase). They can be structured as follows:

I. Makarism proper
   A. Value judgment: μακάριοι ("How honored")
   B. Subject (plural substantive)

II. Grant of honor
   A. Conjunction: ὅτι ("for")
   B. Present or future status

This structure indicates several things. 1) Their plural 3rd person construction indicates their general (and therefore ideal) character. This offers honor, then, to whomever behaves in like manner. 2) The second parts identify the grant of honor for those who act appropriately. 3) The sequence of the two parts is determined by logic (an act followed by its consequence), and the movement of honor (personal behavior to public validation).

It is important to note several points about how and where the evangelist has used these makarisms, their redactional placement. Other than the two summary statements (4:17, 23), the "Sermon on the Mount" is the first of Jesus' public teaching in the Gospel; this places particular emphasis on this series of makarisms as the inauguration of Jesus' message. The makarisms are the opening of the sermon and therefore set the tone for the whole. The first and eighth motivations (5:3, 10) are identical (thus they form an inclusio), are formulated in the present tense, and emphasize participation in the "kingdom"; the second through seventh motivations (5:4–9) are formulated in the future tense.

All of the motivations obviously may be realized within the community, and in this life. The described behaviors cannot be sustained by a hope after death: belonging in the "kingdom," comfort, mercy, the epithet "sons of God," etc., do not obtain in the afterlife, but in the community of faith. The one problematic statement in this regard is 5:8: "for they will see God." But this affirmation comports with the long history of the theophanic tradition: it relates to close relationship with the divine; and it does not require a futuristic interpretation (see e.g.: Exod 24:9–11; Num 12:8; 14:14; Isa 6:5; Jer 29:12–13; Ps 11:7; 17:15; 24:6; 27:4, 8; John 1:18; Rev 22:4) (see Malina 1988:10). 1 Tim 6:15–16, on the other hand, seems to disallow anyone ever seeing God!

A fundamental difficulty arises from the variety of interpretations of the makarisms. They are often still interpreted as formal blessings—"eschatological" or otherwise (e.g., Koch: 7–8; Schweizer: 80–82; Guelich 1976:416; Crosby: 24; Kselman; Kloppenborg; Kingsbury: 100; Vaught: 13; Patte: 67; Fuller: 956). Luz argues: "For Jesus the unconditional, categorical bestowal of grace on people who are in a desperate situation is decisive" (231). Others have interpreted them as "entrance requirements" (e.g., Strecker 1971:259–62). I would argue that if makarisms are fundamentally expressions of honor, then Matt 5:3–12 must be interpreted as a programmatic value statement: the conditions and behaviors which the community regards as honorable (see White: 81–85). An example of this is a Talmudic makarism and reproach in series:

> How honored (אַשְׁרֵי) are you, Aqiba,
> because you were arrested for words of Torah.
> How shameful (אוֹי) are you, Pappos, because you were
> arrested for idle words. (b. Ber. 61b)

Matthew's third person formulations point to the ideal character of the series, in the tradition of the sages. Seeley's analysis already points us in the direction of a present orientation, as well as towards the social setting of the sages (136).

MATTHEW 23:13–36

Determining the extent of the Matthean unit of reproaches is a bit more complex than for the makarisms. As Whedbee notes, the reproach may continue with a variety of secondary forms, e.g.: threats, laments, proverbs, rhetorical questions, or applications to world history (82). Certainly Matthew's speech unit ends with 23:39. But does the formal unit end with 23:31, or 33, or 36, or 39? That 23:32–36 did not belong to an oral form of this reproach series may be deduced from several observations: 23:34 speaks to the future persecution of Christians in the synagogues; 23:35 places culpability on the scribes and Pharisees for all the righteous dead from Abel on down; 23:36 assigns culpability to the whole generation, rather than just scribes and Pharisees; and 23:34–36 derive from the Q tradition (par. Luke 11:49–51). I would argue that the pre-Matthean form probably ended in 23:31. Patte even argues that the present text of Matthew 23 has four distinct parts: "23:1–12 (practice what they tell you, but not what they do); 23:13–31 (the 'woes'); 23:32–36 (Jesus affirms his authority over the Pharisees); 23:37–39 (condemnation of Jerusalem and a promise of restoration)" (320–21).

Six of the seven reproaches in Matt 23:13–31 are structured as follows:

I. Reproach proper
   A. Value judgment: οὐαι ὑμῖν ("Shame on you")
   B. Subject: plural noun/s
II. Reason
   A. Conjunction: ὅτι ("for")
   B. Description of actions

(Some mss add an additional reproach in 23:14 which follows the above form.) The exception to this is the one in 23:16; it is structured:

I. Reproach proper
   A. Value judgment: οὐαι ὑμῖν ("Shame on you")
   B. Subject: plural nouns
II. Reason
   A. Quotation formula: οἱ λέγοντες ("who say")
   B. Quotation proper

An important aspect of these reproaches is that they do not include any formal sentence or threat. Their power, therefore, lies in their success at uncovering shameful behaviors, not in legal or theological adjudication. They are imputations of shame on specific groups: scribes and Pharisees. The similarity of the makarism and reproach structures is striking. It is a confirmation of their formal connection and Matthew's redactional intent.

In terms of content, the reproaches are public challenges to the honor of the scribes and Pharisees. Since the audience is "the crowds" and "his [Jesus'] disciples" (23:1), Jesus is publicly ridiculing the scribes and Pharisees. Their behavior and attitudes are called into question. He labels them as deviants: "hypocrites," "blind guides," "blind fools," "blind ones," and "sons of those who killed the prophets" (see Malina and Neyrey 1989:152–54).

The placement of the reproaches by the evangelist is pivotal: they form the conclusion to the public ministry of Jesus. They are introduced with: "Then Jesus said to the crowds and his disciples" (23:1). Following the series of reproaches, Jesus teaches only his disciples (24:1, 3; 26:1, 8, 10, 20–21, 26, 31, 36, 38, 45). Thus the makarisms in Matthew 5 and reproaches in 23 form an inclusio on Jesus' public ministry. The antithetical character of the makarisms and reproaches is not only formal, but semantic as well (see Fig. #2). The antithetical parallels between the two could hardly be accidental.

FIGURE #2: MATTHEW'S MAKARISMS AND REPROACHES COMPARED

MAKARISMS (Matt 5:3–12)	REPROACHES (Matt 23:13–31)
* honoring	* shaming
* third person formulations	* second person formulations
* addressed to disciples	* addressed to opponents
* opens public ministry	* closes public ministry
* "theirs is the kingdom of the heavens" (3, 10)	* "you shut the kingdom of the heavens" (13)
* "hunger and thirst for righteousness" (6)	* "outwardly appear righteous" (28)
* "merciful . . . receive mercy" (7)	* "neglected mercy" (23)
* "pure of heart" (8a)	* "impure" (27)
* "see God" (8b)	* "swear by God's throne" (22)
* "sons of God" (9)	* "son of Gehenna" (15)
* "so they persecuted the prophets" (12)	* "sons of those who killed the prophets" (31)

The inclusio of makarisms and reproaches provides further evidence that these two forms are antipodal (see Gnilka 1:115). While Luke juxtaposes four makarisms (6:20–23) and four reproaches (6:24–26) in the same speech, Matthew has employed his two series as brackets around Jesus' public teaching. Thus honor and shame provide the polar oppositions which open and close the public ministry. These two units thus provide two sets of value judgments in Jesus' mouth which constitute the positive and negative values of the "kingdom." Their sequence is also important: the makarisms open the public ministry, and the reproaches close it. The makarisms thus encourage aspiring to the positive ideals of the kingdom—which will unfold throughout the story of Jesus' ministry. The reproaches reflect back upon the opposition to Jesus by the Pharisees and scribes.

Figure #3 clarifies the antipodal character of the makarisms and reproaches. It also highlights the distinction between these forms and blessing and cursing.

FIGURE #3: BLESSINGS AND CURSES; MAKARISMS AND CASTIGATION

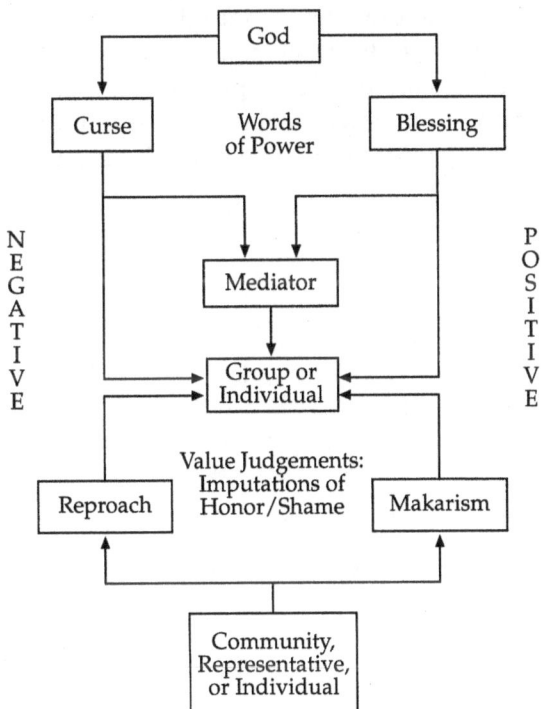

Conclusions

Identifying the makarisms and reproaches throughout the Bible, as well as those in other early Judean and Christian literatures, allows us to see them more clearly in their cultural perspective. Most previous discussions have failed to see their large numbers and their common perspective on honor and shame. The primary conclusions can be summarized as follows: 1) Makarisms and reproaches are thematically related to formal blessings and curses, but linguistically and contextually distinct from them. Consequently, makarisms should not be translated "blessed." The translations of "happy" or "enviable" for the makarisms are also inappropriate since they do not refer to either human emotion or the evil eye. 2) Makarisms and reproaches are value judgments, which can be uttered by sages, prophets, or anyone in the community. They should be translated in keeping with value judgments: the makarisms with "O how honorable" or "How honored"; and the reproaches with "O how shameful" or "Shame on." 3) Makarisms and reproaches are comprehensible only in terms of Mediterranean honor/shame values and the challenge-riposte transactions. Thus they describe and challenge values, but also call for a response. 4) Matt 5:3–10 provides the introduction to Jesus' public ministry and Matt 23:13–31 its conclusion. Consequently they form an honor/shame inclusio around Jesus' public teaching. Furthermore, the evangelist has not only employed them as formal and semantic antitheses, but has paralleled key-words throughout their formulations.

WORKS CITED

Addinall, Peter
    1981   "The Wilderness in Pedersen's Israel." *JSOT* 20:75–83.

Allen, Leslie C.
    1983   *Psalms 101–150*. WBC 21. Waco: Word.

Andersen, F. I.
    1983   "2 (Slavonic Apocalypse of) Enoch." Pp. 91–221 in *The Old Testament Pseudepigrapha*. Vol. 1: *Apocalyptic Literature and Testaments*. Ed. J.H. Charlesworth. Garden City: Doubleday.

Betz, Hans Dieter
    1985   "The Beatitudes of the Sermon on the Mount (Matt. 5:3–12): Observations on Their Literary Form and Theological Significance." Pp. 17–36 in *Essays on the Sermon on the Mount*. Trans. L. L. Welborn. Philadelphia: Fortress.

Boring, M. Eugene
    1985   "Criteria of Authenticity: The Lucan Beatitudes as a Test Case." *Forum* 1/4:3–38.

Bourdieu, Pierre
    1966   "The Sentiment of Honour in Kabyle Society." Pp. 191–241 in Peristiany 1966.

Brichto, Herbert Chanan
    1963   *The Problem of "Curse" in the Hebrew Bible*. SBLMS 13. Philadelphia: Society of Biblical Literature.

Bultmann, Rudolph
    1963   *History of the Synoptic Tradition*. Rev. ed. Trans. J. Marsh. New York: Harper & Row.

Cameron, Rod, ed.
    1982   *The Other Gospels. Non-Canonical Gospel Texts*. Philadelphia: Westminster.

Clifford, Richard J.
    1966   "The Use of הוֹי in the Prophets." *CBQ* 28:458–64.

Corrigan, Gregory M.
    1986   "Paul's Shame for the Gospel." *BTB* 16:23–27.

Crosby, Michael H.
    1981   *Spirituality of the Beatitudes: Matthew's Challenge for First World Christians*. Maryknoll: Orbis.

Dahood, Mitchell
    1970   *Psalms III: 101–150*. AB 17A. Garden City: Doubleday.

Delaney, Carol
1987 "Seeds of Honor, Fields of Shame." Pp. 35-48 in *Honor and Shame and the Unity of the Mediterranean*. Ed. David D. Gilmore. Special Publication of the American Anthropological Association 22. Washington D.C.: American Anthropological Association.

Dodd, C. H.
1968 "The Beatitudes: a form-critical study." Pp. 1–10 in *More New Testament Studies*. Grand Rapids: Eerdmans.

Elliott, John H.
1988 "The Fear of the Lear. The Evil Eye from the Bible to Li'l Abner." *Forum* 4/4:42.
1990 "Paul, Galatians, and the Evil Eye." *CTM* 17:262–73.
1991 "The Evil Eye in the First Testament: The Ecology and Culture of a Pervasive Belief." Pp. 147–59 in *The Bible and the Politics of Exegesis. Essays in Honor of Norman K. Gottwald on His Sixty-Fifth Birthday*. Ed. D. Jobling, et al. Cleveland: Pilgrim.
1992 "Matthew 20:1–15: A Parable of Invidious Comparison and Evil Eye Accusation." *BTB* 22:52–65.

Fensham, F. C.
1962 "Malediction and Benediction in Ancient Near Eastern Vassal Treaties and the Old Testament." *ZAW* 74:1–9.

Finley, M. I.
1979 *The World of Odysseus*. 2nd rev. ed. New York: Viking.

Fitzmyer, Joseph A.
1983 *The Gospel According to Luke I-IX*. 2nd ed. AB 28. Garden City: Doubleday.

Fuller, Reginald H.
1988 "Matthew." Pp. 951–82 in *Harper's Bible Commentary*. Ed. J. L. Mays. San Francisco: Harper & Row.

Gerstenberger, Erhard S.
1962 "The Woe-Oracles in the Prophets." *JBL* 81:249–63.
1988 *Psalms Part 1; With an Introduction to Cultic Poetry*. FOTL 14. Grand Rapids: Eerdmans.

Gilmore, David D.
1987a "Introduction." Pp. 2–21 in Gilmore 1987b.
1987b Ed. *Honor and Shame and the Unity of the Mediterranean*. Special Publication of the American Anthropological Association 22. Washington, D. C.: American Anthropological Association.

Gnilka, Joachim
1986 *Das Matthäusevangelium*. Vol. 1. HTKNT. Freiburg.

Guelich, Robert A.
1976 "The Matthean Beatitudes: 'Entrance Requirements, or 'Eschatological Blessings'?" *JBL* 95:415–34.

1982   *The Sermon on the Mount. A Foundation for Understanding*. Waco: Word.

Gunkel, Hermann
1969   "The Israelite Prophecy from the Time of Amos." Pp. 48–75 in *Twentieth-Century Theology in the Making*. Vol. 1: Themes of Biblical Theology. Ed. J. Pelikan. Trans. R. A. Wilson. New York: Harper & Row [German orig. 1927].

Hals, Ronald M.
1989   *Ezekiel*. FOTL 19. Grand Rapids: Eerdmans.

Hanson, K. C.
1983   *Alphabetic Acrostics: A Form-Critical Study*. Ph.D. Dissertation, Claremont Graduate School. Ann Arbor: University Microfilms.

Harrelson, Walter J.
1962   "Blessing and Cursings." Pp. 446–48 in *Interpreter's Dictionary of the Bible*, vol. 1. Ed. G. A Buttrick. Nashville: Abingdon.

Heller A.
1982   "The Power of Shame." *Dialectical Anthropology* 6:215–28.

Isaac, E.
1983   "1 (Ethiopic Apocalypse of) Enoch." Pp. 5–89 in *The Old Testament Pseudepigrapha*. Vol. 1: *Apocalyptic Literature and Testaments*. Ed. J. H. Charlesworth. Garden City: Doubleday.

Janzen, Waldemar
1965   "אַשְׁרֵי in the Old Testament." *HTR* 58:215–26.
1972   *Mourning Cry and Woe Oracle*. BZAW 125. Berlin: Töpelmann.

Käser, W.
1970   "Beobachtungen zum alttestamentlichen Makarismus." *ZAW* 82:225–50.

Kingsbury, Jack Dean
1985   "Beatitudes." Pp. 100 in *Harper's Bible Dictionary*. Ed. P. J. Achtemeier. San Francisco: Harper & Row.

Klopfenstein, M.
1972   *Scham und Schade nach dem Alten Testament*. ATANT 62. Zurich: Theologischer Verlag.

Kloppenborg, John S.
1986   "Blessing and Marginality. The 'Persecution Beatitude' in Q, Thomas and Early Christianity." *Forum* 2/3:36–56.

Koch, Klaus
1969   *The Growth of the Biblical Tradition. The Form Critical Method*. Trans. S. M. Cupitt. London: Black.

Kodjak, Andrej
1986   *A Structural Analysis of the Sermon on the Mount*. Religion and Reason 34. New York: de Gruyter.

Kraus, Han-Joachim
    1988   *Psalms 1–59: A Commentary*. Trans. H.C. Oswald. Minneapolis: Augsburg.

Kselman, John S.
    1985   "Curse and Blessing." Pp. 198–99 in *Harper's Bible Dictionary*. Ed. P.J. Achtemeir. San Francisco: Harper and Row.

Lambrecht, Jan
    1985   *The Sermon on the Mount. Proclamation and Exhortation*. Good News Studies 14. Wilmington: Glazier.

Lang, Bernhard
    1982   "The Social Organization of Peasant Poverty in Biblical Israel." *JSOT* 24:47–63 [Revised version: Pp. 114–27 in *Monotheism and the Prophetic Minority*. Social World of Biblical Antiquity Series, 1. Sheffield: JSOT Press, 1983].

Layton, Bentley
    1987   "The Book of Thomas: The Contender Writing to the Perfect." Pp. 400–409 in *The Gnostic Scriptures*. Garden City: Doubleday.

Louw, Johannes P. and Eugene A. Nida
    1988   *Greek-English Lexicon of the New Testament Based on Semantic Domains*. Vol. 1. New York: United Bible Societies.

Luz, Ulrich
    1989   *Matthew 1–7: A Commentary*. Trans. W. C. Linss. Continental Commentaries. Minneapolis: Augsburg.

McEleney, Neil J.
    1981   "The Beatitudes of the Sermon on the Mount/Plain." *CBQ* 43:1–13.

Malina, Bruce J.
    1981   *The New Testament World. Insights From Cultural Anthropology*. Atlanta: John Knox.
    1986   "Religion in the World of Paul." *BTB* 16:91–101.
    1988   "Patron and Client: The Analogy Behind Synoptic Theology." *Forum* 4/1:2–32.

Malina, Bruce J. and Jerome H. Neyrey
    1989   *Calling Jesus Names. The Social Value of Labels in Matthew*. Social Facets. Sonoma: Polebridge.
    1991   "Honor and Shame in Luke-Acts: Pivotal Values of the Mediterranean World." Pp. 25–65 in *The Social World of Luke-Acts: Models for Interpretation*. Ed. J.H. Neyrey. Peabody: Hendrickson.

May, David M.
    1987   "Mark 3:20–35 From the Perspective of Shame/Honor." *BTB* 17:83–87.

Meeker, Michael
    1976   "Meaning and Society in the Near East: Examples from the Black Sea Turks and the Levantine Arabs (I)." *International Journal of Middle East Studies* 7:243–70, 383–422.

Moulton, James Hope and George Milligan
    1957   *The Vocabulary of the Greet Testament Illustrated from the Papyri and Other Non-Literary Sources*. 3rd ed. Grand Rapids: Eerdmans.

Mowinckel, Sigmund
    1962   *The Psalms in Israel's Worship*. 2 vols. Trans. D. R. Ap-Thomas. Nashville: Abingdon.

Muenchow, Charles
    1989   "Dust and Dirt in Job 42:6." *JBL* 108:597–611.

Patte, Daniel
    1987   *The Gospel of Matthew. A Structural Commentary on Matthew's Faith*. Philadelphia: Fortress.

Pedersen, Johs.
    1926   *Israel: Its Life and Culture*. Vols. 1–2. Trans. A. Moller. London: Oxford University.

Perdue, Leo G.
    1986   "The Wisdom Sayings of Jesus." *Forum* 2/3:16–18.

Peristiany, J. G., ed.
    1966   *Honour and Shame. The Values of Mediterranean Society*. The Nature of Human Society Series. Chicago: University of Chicago Press.

Pilch, John J.
    1991   *Introducing the Cultural Context of the Old Testament*. Hear the Word, 1. New York: Paulist.

Pitt-Rivers, Julian
    1966   "Honour and Social Status." In Peristiany 1966.
    1977   "The Anthropology of Honour." Pp. 1–17 in *The Fate of Shechem or the Politics of Sex. Essays in the Anthropology of the Mediterranean*. Cambridge Studies and Papers in Social Anthropology. Cambridge: Cambridge University Press.

Porter, J.R.
    1978   "Biblical Classics III: Johs. Pedersen, Israel." *ExpT* 90:36–40.

Rowold, Henry
    1985   "Yahweh's Challenge to Rival: The Form and Function of the Yahweh-Speech in Job 38–39." *CBQ* 47:199–211.

Schneider, C.
    1977   *Shame, Exposure, and Privacy*. Boston: Beacon.

Schweizer, Eduard
    1975   *The Good News According to Matthew*. Trans. D.E. Green. Atlanta: John Knox.

Scott, R.B.Y.
    1957   "The Literary Structure of Isaiah's Oracles." Pp. 175–86 in *Studies in Old Testament Prophecy Presented to Professor Theodore H. Robinson*. Ed. H. H. Rowley. Edinburgh: T. & T. Clark.

Seeley, David
  1991 "Blessings and Boundaries: Interpretations of Jesus' Death in Q." *Semeia* 55:131–46.

Stansell, Gary
  1992 "Honor and Shame in the David Narratives." Pp. 94–114 in *Was Ist Der Mensch ...? Beiträge zur Anthropologie des Alttestaments*. Ed. F. Crüsemann, et al. Munich: Chr. Kaiser.

Strecker, Georg
  1971 "Die Makarismen der Bergpredigt." *NTS* 17:255–75.
  1988 *The Sermon on the Mount. An Exegetical Commentary*. Trans. O. C. Dean, Jr. Nashville: Abingdon.

Talbert, Charles H.
  1982 *Reading Luke. A Literary and Theological Commentary on the Third Gospel*. New York: Crossroad.

Tilborg, Sjef van
  1986 *The Sermon on the Mount as an Ideological Intervention. A Reconstruction of Meaning*. Assen: Van Gorcum.

Tucker, Gene M.
  1985 "Prophecy and the Prophetic Literature." Pp. 325–68 in *The Hebrew Bible and Its Modern Interpreters*. Ed. D.A. Knight and G.M. Tucker, eds. The Bible and Its Modern Interpreters 1. Philadelphia: Fortress.

Vaught, Carl G.
  1986 *The Sermon on the Mount. A Theological Interpretation*. SUNY Series in Religious Studies. Albany, NY: State University of New York.

Wanke, Günther
  1966 "אוֹי und הוֹי." *ZAW* 78:215–18.

Westermann, Claus
  1967 *Basic Forms of Prophetic Speech*. Trans. H.C. White. Philadelphia: Westminster.
  1974 "Der Gebrauch von אַשְׁרֵי im Alten Testament." Pp. 191–95 in *Forschung am Alten Testament. Gesammelte Studien* 2. ThBü 55. München: Chr. Kaiser.
  1978 *Blessing in the Bible and the Life of the Church*. Trans. K. Crim. OBT 2. Philadelphia: Fortress.

Whedbee, J. William
  1971 *Isaiah and Wisdom*. Nashville: Abingdon.

White, Leland J.
  1985 "Grid and Group in Matthew's Community: The Righteousness/Honor Code in the Sermon on the Mount." *Semeia* 35:61–90.

Wolff, Hans Walter
  1934 "Die Begründungen der prophetischen Heils- und Unheilssprüche." *ZAW* 52:1–22.

1973 *Amos the Prophet. The Man and His Background.* Trans. F.R. McCurley. Philadelphia: Fortress.

1977 *Joel and Amos. A Commentary on the Books of the Prophets Joel and Amos.* Trans. W. Janzen, et al. Hermeneia. Philadelphia: Fortress.

Wright, G. Ernest

1964 *Isaiah.* Layman's Bible Commentaries. London: SCM.

DESPISING THE SHAME OF THE CROSS: HONOR AND SHAME IN THE JOHANNINE PASSION NARRATIVE

Jerome H. Neyrey

ABSTRACT

The passion narrative in John 18–19 is profitably viewed in terms of the values of honor and shame. A model of this anthropological concept is presented, which stresses the form of the typical honor challenge (claim, challenge, riposte, and public verdict). This model then serves as a template for reading John 18–19 to bring the phenomena of honor and shame to the surface in that narrative and to interpret the endless confrontations described there in their appropriate cultural perspective. Thus from the narrator's point of view, Jesus maintains his honor and even gains more in his death; he is in no way shamed by the events.

I. INTRODUCTION

New Testament authors reflect the general perception of crucifixion in the Greco-Roman world as "shame" (Heb 12:2). Various classical authors give us a sense of the typical process of crucifixion, which at every step entailed progressive humiliation of the victim and loss of honor (Hengel: 22–32):

1. Crucifixion was considered the appropriate punishment for slaves (Cicero, *In Verrem* 2.5.168), bandits (Jos. *War* 2.253), prisoners of war (Jos. *War* 5.451) and revolutionaries (Jos. *Ant.* 17.295; see Hengel 1977:46–63).

2. Public trials ("misera est ignominia iudicorum publicorum," Cicero, *Pro Rabinio* 9–17) served as status degradation rituals, which labelled the accused as a shameful person.

3. Flogging and torture, especially the blinding of eyes and the shedding of blood, generally accompanied the sentence (Jos. *War* 5.449–51 & 3.321; Livy 22.13.19; 28.37.3; Seneca, *On Anger* 3.6; Philo, *Flac.* 72; Diod. Sic. 33.15.1; Plato, *Gorgias* 473bc & *Republic* 2.362e). Since, according to *m. Mak.* 3.12, scourging was done both to the front and back of the body, the victims were nude; often they befouled themselves with urine or excrement (3.14).

4. The condemned were forced to carry the cross beam (Plutarch, *Delay* 554B).

5. The victim's property, normally clothing, was confiscated; hence they were further shamed by being denuded (see Diod. Sic. 33.15.1).

6. The victim lost power and thus honor through pinioning of hands and arms, especially the mutilation of being nailed to the cross (Philo, *Post.* 61; *Somn.* 2.213).

7. Executions served as crude forms of public entertainment, where the crowds ridiculed and mocked the victims (Philo, *Sp. Leg.* 3.160), who were sometimes affixed to crosses in an odd and whimsical manner, including impalement (Seneca: *Consol. ad Marciam* 20.3; Josephus, *War* 5.451).

8. Death by crucifixion was often slow and protracted. The powerless victim suffered bodily distortions, loss of bodily control, and enlargement of the penis (Steinberg 1983:82–108). Ultimately they were deprived of life and thus the possibility of gaining satisfaction or vengeance.

9. In many cases, victims were denied honorable burial; corpses were left on display and devoured by carrion birds and scavenger animals (Pliny, *H.N.* 36.107–108).

Victims would thus experience themselves as progressively humiliated and stripped entirely of public respect or honor.

The issue, however, lies not in the brutal pain endured. For among the warrior elite, at least, the endurance of pain and suffering were marks of ἀνδρεία or manly courage (e.g., Hercules' labors; Paul's hardship catalogues, e.g., 2 Cor 6:3–10; 11:23–33). Silence of the victim during torture was a mark of honor (see Isa 53:7; Cicero, *In Verrem* 2.5.162; Josephus, *War* 6.304). But mockery, loss of respect, and humiliation were the bitter parts; the loss of honor, the worst fate. Although the gospels record in varying degrees the physical torture of Jesus, they focus on the various attempts to dishonor him by spitting on him (Mark 14:65//Matt 26:67; see Mark 10:33–34), striking him in the face and head (Mark 14:65//Matt 26:67), ridiculing him (ἐμπαίζειν: Mark 15:20, 31; Matt 27:29, 31, 41), heaping insults upon him (ὀνειδίζειν: Mark 15:32, 34; Matt 27:44), and treating him as though he were nothing (ἐξουθενεῖν, Luke 23:11; see Acts 4:11).

This study of the Johannine passion narrative views it precisely through the lenses of honor and shame. We suggest that despite all the shameful treatment of Jesus, he is portrayed, not only as maintaining his honor, but even gaining glory and prestige (Malina and Neyrey 1988:95–131). Far from being a status degradation ritual, his passion is seen as a status elevation ritual. This hypothesis entails a larger consideration, namely, the importance of honor and shame as pivotal values of the Mediterranean world (Malina 1981:25). We presume that the original audience would have perceived Jesus' passion in these terms.

Modern readers, however, are not cognizant of these pivotal cultural values. We neither understand the grammar of honor nor appreciate the social dynamics in which they play so important a part. If we would interpret the narrative of Jesus' death from the appropriate cultural point of view, we must attempt to see things through the lenses of ancient Mediterranean culture, which were those of honor and shame. In the cultural world of the New Testament, Jesus' death by crucifixion was acknowledged as a most shameful experience. Paul merely expressed what others perceived when he labelled the crucified Christ as a σκάνδαλον to Jews and μωρία to Greeks (1 Cor 1:23). The author of Hebrews explicitly calls the cross "shame" (αἰσχύνες, 12:2).

The gospels acknowledge that prophets are denied honor in their own villages (ἄτιμος, Mark 6:4//Matt 13:57). They tell of messengers sent to a vineyard, who are wounded in the head and treated shamefully (ἐτίμασαν, Mark 12:4). But the early Christians counted this type of public shame as honor: "... rejoicing that they were counted worthy to suffer dishonor (ἀτιμασθῆναι) for the name" (Acts 5:41). Honor and shame, then, are not only integral parts of the language patterns which describe the fate of Jesus and his disciples, but a basic element in the way the Christian story perceives and deals with suffering, rejection, and death.

II. A BRIEF GRAMMAR OF HONOR AND SHAME

Greeks, Romans, and Judeans all considered honor and shame to be pivotal values in their cultures (Adkins; Malina 1981; Gilmore). From Homer to Herodotus and from Pindar to Paul (Nagy: 222–242; Friedrich: 290), men lived and died in quest of honor, reputation, fame, approval, and respect. Lexical definitions offer a wide range of overlapping meanings for honor/τιμή: (1) the price or value of something, (2) respect paid to someone, (3) honorary office, (4) dignity or status, (5) honors or awards given someone (Schneider: 169–71). Paul Friedrich offers a social grammar of honor based on Greek epic poetry: "The structure of Iliadic honor can be stated in part as a larger network that includes propositions about honor and nine honor-linked values: power, wealth, magnanimity, personal loyalty, 'precedence,' sense of shame, fame or 'reputation,' courage, and excellence" (290).

A detailed grammar of honor can be found in Malina's *New Testament World* in our co-authored essay of 1991, but a summary of it may aid readers unfamiliar with the topic. Honor comes to someone either by *ascription* by another (birth, adoption, appointment) or by one's own *achievement*. Achieved honor derives from benefaction (Luke 7:5; Diod. Sic., 6.1.2), military prowess, success at athletic games, and the like. In the warrior culture of Greece and Rome, honor accrues with prowess in battle (see David and Goliath) or endurance in labors (Heracles; see 2 Tim 4:7–8). Yet most commonly honor is acquired in the face-to-face game of challenge and riposte which makes up much of the daily life of individuals in villages and cities.

Honor resides in one's name, always an inherited name. Sons enjoy the honor of their father's name and membership in his clan. Hence, they are regularly identified as "the son of so-and-so" (e.g., 1 Sam 9:1–2; Ezra 7:1–6). Yet individuals might be called by honorific names such as "Rabbi" (Matt 23:7) or "Prophet" (John 9:17) or "Christ" (John 7:26). These labels, which are claims to precedence and honor, are likely to be bitterly contested.

Honor resides in certain public roles, statuses, and offices. Fathers enjoy great honor in their households, honor which is sanctioned in the Ten Commandments. Most notably, honor was attached to offices such as king and high priest, as well as governor, proconsul, and other civic or imperial offices. In the great tradition of the aristocrats, the hierarchical ranking of honor was clearly known (Garnsey: 221–71). But in the little tradition of peasants and artisans, such ranking was a matter of considerable debate and controversy, which we can observe in the squabbles over the seating at dinner tables (Luke 14:7–11).

Honor has "a strong material orientation" (Schneider: 170). That is, honor is expressed and measured by one's possessions which must be on display. Wealth in general denotes honor—not simply the possession of wealth, but its consumption and display: e.g., banquets, fine clothes, weapons, houses, etc. Hence it is not surprising to hear Josephus describing as "honor" the benefactions Vespasian bestowed on him: "raiment and other precious gifts" (*War* 3.408). Similarly he describes the honors given Daniel: "(The king) gave him purple to wear and put a chain of linked gold about his neck" (*Ant.* 10.240). Finally Josephus records Haman's suggestion to the Persian king concerning how to honor a friend: "If you wish to cover with glory the man whom you say you love, let him ride on horseback wearing the same dress as yourself, with a necklace of gold, and let one of your close friends precede him and proclaim throughout the whole city that this is the honour shown to him whom the king honours" (*Ant.* 11.254).

Anthropologists describe the physical body as a microcosm of the social body (Douglas: 115). The values and rules pertinent to the macrocosm are replicated in the way the physical body is perceived and treated. Let us examine how the body replicates honor. 1. *The head and face* are particular loci of personal honor and respect. A head is honored when crowned or anointed. Servants and courtiers honor a monarch by avoiding looking them in the face, that is, by the deep bow. Comparably, to slap someone on the mouth, spit in their face, box their ears or strike their heads shames this member and so gives "affront" (Matt 26:67; Luke 22:63–64; Mark 15:17–20). 2. *Clothing* covers the dishonorable or shameful parts of the body (1 Cor 12:23–24), namely the genitals and the buttocks. Clothing, moreover, symbolizes honor: "Men are the glory of God and their clothes are the glory of men" (*Derek Eretz Zuta*). Elites signal their status by their clothing and adornment (Luke 7:25; see *m. Yoma* 7.5). Purple clothing was a particular mark of honor, worn by kings (Judg 8:26), priests (Exod 28:4–6; 39:1, 28–29; 1 Macc 10:20; 11:58), and nobles at court (Ezek 23:6; Esth 8:6; Dan 5:7; see Reinhold: 7–21, 48–61). Uniforms signal rank or office. Philo provides a striking example of the way clothing replicates honor in his description of Pharaoh's investiture of Joseph with symbols of status giving him a "...royal seat, sacred robe, golden necklace, setting him on his second chariot, bade him go the round of the city with a crier walking in front who proclaimed the appointment" (*Jos.* 120). The costuming of Jesus in a purple robe and a crown of thorns mocks him with the normal trappings of honor. Being stripped of clothing, moreover, eliminates all marks of honor and status; it also indicates a loss of power to cover and defend one's "shameful parts." 3. *Bodily postures* express honor. Masters sit at table, while servants stand and wait upon them (Luke 17:7–8; see 13:29). Twenty-four elders stand around the throne where God is seated; they fall down before him in worship (Rev 4:10). Προσκυνεῖν describes a posture whereby someone bends low to kiss another, either on the hand or the foot; thus it comes to mean bowing before or showing respect for someone (Josephus, *Ant.* 11.209).

Yet in the perception of the ancients, honor, like all other goods, existed in quite limited supply (Foster: 304–5). There was only so much gold, so much strength, so much honor available. When someone achieved honor, it was thought to be at the expense of others. Philo, for example, condemns polytheism, because in honoring others as deities, the honor due to the true God is diminished: "God's honour is set at naught by those who deify mortals" (*Ebr.* 110; see Josephus, *Ant.* 4.32; *War* 1.559). When John's disciples lament to their master that Jesus is gaining more disciples and honor, they understand that Jesus' gain must be John's loss. John confirms this, "He must increase, but I must decrease" (John 3:30). Thus, claims to honor by one person will tend to be perceived as threats to the honor of others, and consequently need to be challenged, not acknowledged. In fact, two Gospels state that it was out of envy that Jesus' enemies handed him over (Mark 15:10//Matt 27:18; cf. John 11:47–48).

Φιλοτιμία or love of honor was a powerful driving force in antiquity. We are particularly interested in how this was played out in the rather ordinary circumstances of life. Honor must be both claimed and acknowledged. After all, it is the respect one has in the eyes of others. But honor claims are vulnerable to challenge. Challenges must be met with an appropriate riposte or honor is lost. All such claims, challenges, and ripostes take place in the public domain, and their verdict of success or failure determines the outcome of these games (Malina 1981:30–33; Malina and Neyrey 1991a:36–38, 49–51). Claim, challenge, riposte and verdict, then, constitute the formal elements in the endless contests for honor and respect.

Thus far we have discussed "honor," but we must be equally aware of "shame." Contempt, loss of face, defeat, and ridicule all describe shame, the loss of honor. The grammar of honor presented above can be reversed to describe "shame." Shame can be *ascribed* or *achieved*. A magistrate may ascribe shame by declaring one guilty and so worthy of public flogging (2 Cor 11:23–25); a king may mock and treat one with contempt (Luke 23:11). God may declare one a "Fool!" (Luke 12:20). Thus the elite and those in power may declare one honorless and worthy of contempt: ". . . exclude, revile, and cast out your name as evil" (Luke 6:22). Yet shame may be *achieved* by one's folly or by cowardice and failure to respond to a challenge. One may refuse to participate in the honor-gaining games characteristic of males, and thus bring contempt on oneself.

The bodily grammar for honor works also for shame. If the honorable parts of the body, the head and face, are struck, spat upon, slapped, blindfolded, or otherwise maltreated, shame ensues. If the right arm, symbol of male power and strength, is bound, tied, or nailed, the resulting powerlessness denotes shame. If one is publicly stripped naked, flogged, paraded before the crowds, and led through the streets, one is shamed. Shame results when one's blood is intentionally spilled, but especially when one is killed by another.

III. IRONY: TURNING SHAME INTO HONOR

Since there are two parties competing in the passion narrative, there are two perceptions of what is occurring. The enemies of Jesus bind, slap, spit upon, blindfold, flog, strip, and kill Jesus; their actions are all calculated to "mock" and "revile" him. In their eyes they have shamed Jesus. But the gospel, while it records these actions and gestures of shame, tells quite a different story. In the evangelist's eyes, Jesus' shame and humiliation is truly the account of his glory: "Ought not the Christ suffer and so enter into his glory?" (Luke 24:26; see Acts 14:22; Heb 2:10). Indeed, in the Fourth Gospel, his death is regularly described as glory and glorification (John 7:39; 12:28; 17:5; see 21:19). Or, to paraphrase Paul, foolishness, weakness, and shame in human eyes are wisdom, strength, and honor in God's eyes (1 Cor 1:20, 25). Thus the story of Jesus' shame is ironically understood by his disciples as his "lifting up," his exaltation, his enthronement, in short, his honor. The issue might be rephrased: Who gets to judge whether the crucifixion is honor or shame? If the public verdict rests with the Judeans, then Jesus is shamed. But if the community of believers renders the verdict on the basis of God's riposte or Jesus' demonstration of power in death, then the verdict is of honor.

This ironic perspective is part and parcel of the principle that Jesus constantly narrates: that last is first, least is greatest, dead is alive, shame is honor (Duke 1985:95–116, 126–38). Hence, two perspectives need to be distinguished as we read the account of Jesus' crucifixion: in the eyes of outsiders and enemies, his crucifixion is unqualified shame! But in the eyes of his disciples, it is ironic honor. Let us now take these abstract notions of honor (and shame) and use them as an exciting and illuminating lens for perceiving the passion narrative of Jesus, the honorable one.

IV. HONOR AND SHAME IN JOHN 18–19

1. *Arrest (18:1–11)*. Although capture and arrest normally denote dishonor, this narrative presents a scene of honor displayed and maintained. First of all, honor means power and control (de la Potterie, 1989: 29). In this regard, when the cohort approaches Jesus, he steps forward to take charge of the situation. By claiming that "Jesus knew all that was to befall him" (18:4), the narrator signals Jesus' control of the situation (see 19:28). Moreover, he questions the powerful forces gathered against him: "Whom do you seek?" In the cultural scenario of honor and shame, the questioner generally acts in the challenging or commanding position (see Mark 11:27–33).

At his remark, "I am he," the soldiers "drew back and fell to the ground" (18:6), leaving Jesus standing. Honor is thus signalled by bodily posture. Commentators regularly note that Jesus' "I AM" can be read as the divine name which he is granted to use (Neyrey 1988:213–20). Falling to the ground characterizes human reactions in the presence of the glory of God (Ezek 1:28; 44:4) or at least an honor-bestowing posture in the presence of a superior person (Dan 2:46; Rev 1:17). At a minimum, Jesus enjoys such a prominent and honorable status that armies fall at his feet. Even if Dodd is correct that the narrator is drawing on psalms describing how one's foes stumble and fall when attacking (Dodd: 76–77), nevertheless some vindication or riposte to a challenge is evident. If this language describes Jesus' heavenly status, then he enjoys the same honor as God, an honor that God commands (5:23). To use God's name, "I AM," might be considered an act of power; and honor is always attached to power.

The narrator repeats the sequence of events in 18:7-8, which doubles the impression of Jesus' strength and honor. His control of the situation extends even to his command about the safe departure of his disciples: "Let these others go" (18:8). Weak people do not tell a cohort of Roman soldiers what to do. This proves, moreover, that his word of honor is true and trustworthy: "This was to fulfil the word which he had spoken, 'I did not lose a single one of those you gave me'" (18:9). Thus the narrator presents Jesus firmly in control: knowing all that will happen, asking questions, controlling the events, giving commands, and receiving profound respect from his would-be assailants. He is without doubt the most honorable person in the situation.

Jesus' commanding posture reminds the reader of the Noble Shepherd discourse, where he disavowed that he was a victim and claimed power even over death: "No one takes my life from me, but I lay it down of my own accord. I have power to lay it down, and I have power to take it again" (10:18). Since power is one of the public faces of honor, Jesus' power to protect his sheep as well as his power to lay down his life indicate that he suffers no shame whatever here. Nothing happens against his will, so he is in no way diminished.

Yet others in the narrative see the scene differently. Simon Peter drew his sword and struck at one of the arresting crowd, which we must interpret as his riposte to the perceived challenge to Jesus' honor. In other circumstances, his action would be labelled an honorable thing, namely, the defense of one's leader against an honor challenge. Jesus himself states this: "If my kingdom were of this world, my servants would fight, that I not be handed over to the Jews" (18:36). Normally failure to respond to a challenge is shameful, but here Jesus explains that it is precisely out of honor that he refuses to resist, that is, out of respect for the will of his Father: "Shall I not drink the cup which the Father has given me?" (18:11). Peter's riposte, then, is unnecessary, for Jesus' honor is not threatened. Indeed, it belongs to the virtue of ἀνδρεία or courage to endure what must be endured (Seeley: 117–41). And courage of this sort is an honorable thing.

2. *Jewish Investigation (18:12–14, 19–24)*. Outsiders see only that Jesus has lost power: "The cohort seized Jesus and bound him" (18:12). His captors take him to the private chambers of Annas, a very powerful enemy, who questions Jesus. Recall that questions are generally challenges. Here Jesus delivers a bold response: "I have spoken openly to the world; I have always taught in the synagogues and in the temple, where all Jews come together" (18:20). Jesus claims that he has acted as an honorable

man, always appearing in the appropriate male space, the public arena, and speaking boldly and clearly. His παρρησία (bold speech) denotes courageous and honorable public behavior (see 1 Thess 2:2). In contrast, this Gospel declares as shameful people who are afraid to speak openly about the Christ (9:22–23; 12:42; see Phil 1:20).

The narrative interprets Jesus' bold speech as a riposte to Annas' challenging questions. Jesus commands his interrogator, "Ask those who have heard me. They know what I said" (18:21). This occasions a severe counter-challenge from one of the officers standing by, who "struck Jesus with his hand" (v. 22; see 19:3). The gesture was surely a slap in the face, thus giving an "affront" to Jesus. It is similar to the blows given Jesus according to the synoptic accounts (Matt 26:67; Mark 14:65; Luke 22:63–64; see Matt 5:39). But Jesus is not silenced or humbled as was Paul, when he was struck by Annas' servant (Acts 23:4–5). He gives an appropriate riposte, "If I have spoken wrongly, bear witness to the wrong; but if I have spoken rightly, why do you strike me?" (18:23). Thus he withstands the insult and continues to speak boldly; he has the last word.

3. *Roman Trial (18:28–19:16).* The very fact of being put on trial is itself an honor challenge, simply because the one who is publicly accused experiences his claims to honor (name, worth, reputation) to be publicly questioned. Modern people have idealized trials as occasions not only to clear one's name, but to put the system itself on trial, that is, to challenge the challenger. Our judicial process, moreover, functions on the presumption of innocence. Not so the ancients, where guilt was presumed. It was inherently shameful to be seized and publicly charged with wrongdoing, "If this man were not an evildoer, we would not have handed him over to you" (18:30).

The trial episode (18:28–19:16) can be described as an extended game of charge and refutation or challenge and riposte. This occurs on several levels. First, those who deliver Jesus engage in their own challenge-riposte game with Pilate. Pilate *claims* the honor of procurator and magistrate as he questions them ("What accusation?" 18:29); they *challenge* him by asserting their own power ("If this man were not an evildoer . . ." v. 30); and this leads to Pilate's *riposte* ("Take him yourselves . . . ." v. 31). For the moment Pilate wins, as they are forced to admit that they have no power: "It is not lawful for us . . ." (v. 31). This challenge-riposte game between Pilate and the Judeans will be continued in 18:39–40 and 19:6, 12–16. But the main contest focusses on the formal process of Jesus before Pilate, which also is an elaborate game of challenge and riposte.

Commentators note the alternation of scenes in the trial from outside to inside, and even the chiastic shape of the narrative. Raymond Brown

(859) provides the following arrangement (for minor variations, cf. Giblin 1986:223).

1. *Outside* (xviii 28–32)
   Jews demand death

2. *Inside* (xviii 33–38a)
   Pilate questions Jesus
   about kingship

3. *Outside* (xviii 38b-40)
   Pilate finds Jesus not guilty;
   choice of Barabbas

4. *Inside* (xix 1–3)
   Soldiers scourge Jesus

7. *Outside* (xix 12–16a)
   Jews obtain death

6. *Inside* (xix 9–11)
   Pilate talks with Jesus
   about power

5. *Outside* (xix 4–8)
   Pilate finds Jesus not guilty;
   "Behold the man"

Commentators are wont to contrast these scenes as "public" (outside) and "private" (inside). Yet the designation "private/inside" is misleading here, for we should not imagine Pilate and Jesus having a tete-a-tete. And even if the narrative action occurs "within" the Roman compound, it is still a "public" place occupied by Roman soldiers, and not the "private" world of the household (cf. 12:1–8; 13:3–5). Dodd's remark that there are two stages, "a front stage and a back" (96), seems more accurate. Yet the narrative distinction between "going within" and "going out" serves to mark the various scenes and different audiences. The "outside" public scenes are the honor contests between Pilate and the Judeans. The so-called "inside" scenes, which comprise the *cognitio* of the trial between judge and the accused, are also public in that they occur in the public forum of the Roman courtyard or praetorium, whether this be the fortress Antonia (Josephus, *Ant.* 15.292) or the new palace of Herod (Benoit 1952:545–49). The "outside" crowds are informed of the results of the "inside" contest, which affects their challenge-riposte game with Pilate. The honor-shame dynamic, then, occurs on both stages, but between different sets of contestants.

Trials under Roman jurisdiction have a formal structure which is helpful to note (Sherwin-White: 12–20; Neyrey 1987:509–11):

Formal Elements of a Roman Trial	1st	2nd
1. arrest	18:1–11	-------
2. charges	18:28–32	19:7
3. judge's cognitio.	18:33–38a	19:8–11
4. verdict	18:38b	19:12
5. judicial warning	19:1–6	-------
6. sentence	-------	19:13–16

This structure indicates that Jesus' trial went through two forensic cycles; it helps, moreover, to clarify the roles of Pilate, Jesus, and the crowds, especially in terms of the four formal elements of an honor contest. The crowds, who function as the witnesses or accusers in the forensic process, *challenge* Jesus' *claims*. Pilate, the judge, examines these challenges and determines whether Jesus' claims are honorable or not. Jesus, who is on trial, is challenged precisely as to his honorable status. Let us now view in greater detail these forensic elements and roles in terms of honor and shame.

Charges (18:29–33). This gospel mentions that Roman soldiers participated in the seizure of Jesus (18:3); their presence indicates that Jesus was in some sense arrested. The charges against him which Pilate investigates are formal challenges to his claims to honor and status: "Are you the *King of the Jews?*" (18:33; see also 19:7, 14, 19). From the beginning, Jesus has been acclaimed as a most honorable person, and so enjoys a singular portion of ascribed honor. On the basis of God's own prompting, John the Baptizer acclaimed him "Son of God" (1:34). Disciples acknowledge him as "the Messiah" (1:41) and "Son of God and King of Israel" (1:49). Even a leader of the Judeans accepts him as "a teacher come from God" (3:2). According to the story, various people acclaim him "savior of the world" (4:42), "prophet" (6:14; 9:17), "king" (6:15; 12:13–15), and "Christ" (7:26). In the game of honor and shame, all of this constitutes a claim of honor, the public identity and reputation of Jesus, which is now being challenged in this trial.

Cognitio (18:33–38). The judge's *cognitio* of Jesus in his judicial quarters serves as the forum where Jesus' honor claims are both *challenged* and *defended*. On the level of rhetoric, Pilate asks questions which challenge Jesus, whose riposte is initially the clever strategy of answering a question with a question (see Mark 11:28–33; 12:14–16). Pilate challenges with a question: "Are you the King of the Jews?" Jesus parries with his own question: "Do you say this of your own accord . . . ?" Pilate asks more questions: "Am I a Jew?. . . What have you done?. . .So you are a king then?. . . What is truth?" On the narrative level, then, Pilate is perceived as asserting his own honor claims as the embodiment of Roman authority by his rhetorical posture as the figure whose duty it is to ask questions and so challenge others. This initial exchange sparkles with honor challenges. Pilate asks a question, presumably concerning the charge against Jesus. By questioning Pilate, Jesus might be said to be giving a riposte: "Do you say this of your own accord . . ." (v. 34). Pilate's response is not only scorn ("Am I a Jew?"), but a mockery of Jesus. How shameful, he points out, that "Your own nation and the chief priests have handed you over" (v. 35).

This sparring game quickly fades, for the narrator wishes to portray Jesus giving a solemn *riposte* to the challenge to his identity and authority. "Kingship" is Pilate's challenge, a very noble and honorable status, which Jesus defends. Twice he proclaims, "My kingship is not of this world" (18:36, 37). If his kingship is not of this world, it must belong to another world (8:23), that is, God's world, which is eternal, unchanging, and truly honorable. Although this "world" was once a worthy recipient of divine favor (3:16; 4:42; 10:36; 12:47), it quickly proved hostile to Jesus. He became an alien here in this world and met only challenge and opposition (1:9–10; Meeks 1972:67–70). The world's hostility, then, constitutes an ongoing challenge to Jesus' honor. But the assertion that his kingdom is not of this world implies that he belongs to a better kingdom, which must triumph over the hostility experienced here. Although challenged, Jesus belongs to a kingdom where he is honored as he should be (5:23; 17:5, 24).

This Gospel speaks of a ruler of this world, who will be Jesus' chief challenger. But even this powerful figure "has no power over me" (14:30); he will be cast out (12:31) and judged (16:11). Thus Jesus boasted to his disciples, "I have overcome the world" (16:30). This powerful challenger appears to be Satan (Schnackenburg: 2.391). But as the passion narrative progresses, even the Roman emperor will qualify as a rival of God (19:12, 15). Yet if Jesus' kingship were of this world, his followers would do the honorable thing and "fight, that I not be handed over to the Jews" (18:36). The vindicator of his kingship, then, must be a most powerful person also "not of this world," namely God. He will give the riposte for King Jesus (12:28; 17:1). But the claim that Jesus is a king remains unassailable: "You say that I am a king; for this I was born, and for this I have come into the world" (18:37). Jesus makes another *claim* that pertains to his kingship, "Every one who is of the truth hears my voice" (v. 37). This directly echoes the remarks about the shepherd in 10:3–4, 26–27 (Meeks 1967:66–67). If "shepherd" is a metaphor for king (i.e., David, the Royal Shepherd), then Jesus reaffirms his honor as king. Good and honorable people, he says, acknowledge this honor claim by "hearing my voice." Whether scornful or cynical (Brown: 869), Pilate's retort, "What is truth?" indicates that he rejects this claim.

Verdict (18:38b). The source of Jesus' honor, while not made explicit here, will shortly be made clear to the court (19:8–11). Yet the reader knows that Jesus enjoys maximum ascribed honor from the most honorable being in the universe, namely, God (see 5:36–38; 12:27–28). All that Jesus is, has, and does comes from God (5:19–29). The reader knows that he comes from God and is returning to God (13:1–3; 17:1–5), where he will be glorified with the glory he had before the creation of the world. At this point in the trial, Jesus has given an adequate riposte to the challenge to his honor; he is a king and defends that claim. On the narrative level, Pilate's forensic verdict of innocence tells the reader, at least, that Jesus' claims are publicly judged to be honorable: "I find no crime in him" (18:38). Honor defended is honor maintained. Yet the public verdict in this honor contest remains unclear.

In acknowledging a custom, Pilate offers to those who have just challenged Jesus' honor the release of this same "King of the Jews" (18:39). This should be interpreted as Pilate's personal challenge to the crowd (Rensberger: 92–94). Their challenge to Jesus had just been rejected (v. 38), and now Pilate taunts them by inviting them to accept Jesus in the fullness of his honor claim, "Will you have me release to you the 'King of the Jews'?" (v. 39). Pilate asks Jesus' challengers publicly to accept a riposte to their challenge, and so admit defeat in this game. His question, then, continues the honor-shame contest between him and the crowds (see 18:29–31). Yet, the crowds give a counter-challenge to Jesus' honor claim and Pilate's gambit: "Not this man!" The shame of being disowned by one's own occurs again (v. 35); Jesus' enemies prefer the release of Barabbas, a thief or social bandit, to him (18:40). The contest between Pilate and the crowd continues as a stalemate.

Judicial Warning (19:1–5). Pilate gives Jesus a "judicial warning," such as Paul received when five times lashed and three times beaten with rods (2 Cor 11:24–25; cf. Acts 5:41). Judicial warnings were intended to inflict pain but especially to humiliate and so discredit troublemakers. In essence, Jesus is beaten and mocked. Even if the technical terms "mock" and "mockery" do not occur here (cf., $\dot{\epsilon}\mu\pi\alpha\dot{\iota}\zeta\epsilon\iota\nu$ Matt 27:29; Mark 15:20; Meeks 1967:69), native readers whose world is structured around honor and shame know what is going on. In the honor culture of ancient warriors, stoic endurance of physical pain denotes courage and honor ($\dot{\alpha}\nu\delta\rho\epsilon\dot{\iota}\alpha$). But to be mocked is by far more painful than the physical beating because it produces the most dreaded of all experiences, shame.

As regards his body, Jesus is shamed by being stripped naked, bound, and beaten in the public forum of the Roman soldiers. His head, the most honorable member of his body, is mocked with a "plaited crown of thorns." His body is dressed in purple, the royal color. Many of the soldiers "struck him with their hands," surely on the face or head, and sarcastically acclaimed his honor, "Hail, King of the Jews" (19:3). Each of these ritual gestures has been shown to be a characteristic element in the honoring of Persian and Roman rulers (Alföldi: $\pi\rho\sigma\kappa\upsilon\nu\eta\sigma\iota\varsigma$/bending the knee: 11–16, 45–70; acclamation, especially as *dominus*: 38–45, 209–10; crown: 17–18, 128–129, 263–67; clothing: 143–56, 175–84, 268–70; scepter: 156–57, 228–35; throne: 140–41, 159–61). Thus a mock coronation ritual occurs (Blank: 62; Meeks 1967:69–72), whose primary function is to shame Jesus, the alleged King of the Judeans.

But if the actors in the drama are portrayed as shaming Jesus, it does not follow that readers of this gospel must concur. On the contrary, insiders have been repeatedly schooled in irony to see Jesus' death as his "being lifted" to heaven (3:14; 8:23; 12:32) or his "glorification" (12:23; 13:31–32; 17:1, 5). The grain of wheat dies and falls into the ground, but thereby lives and bears fruit. In short, the gospel inculcates an ironic point of view that death and shame mean glory and honor. The mock coronation of Jesus, which in the eyes of outsiders means shame, truly betokens honor from the viewpoint of insiders. In terms of Jesus' honor, it truly is a status elevation ritual. Although ironically invested with imperial honors, Jesus nonetheless is acclaimed as honorable, especially in his shame (Duke: 132–33). Rensberger describes this scene as Pilate's humiliation of the Judeans by the sarcastic presentation of a Roman's interpretation of Jewish messianic hopes (93–94).

New Charges/New Cognitio (19:7, 9–11). Pilate then brings forth this Jesus who has been mocked and dishonored. I do not know when modern readers started thinking that such a presentation was supposed to inspire sympathy for Jesus, because in the culture of the time such a scene would surely provoke laughter and derision. Crowds regularly gathered at public executions to participate in the mockery (see Matt 27:38, 39, 41). The crowds react here in culturally predictable ways by continuing their dishonoring of Jesus: "Crucify him! crucify him!" (19:6). Rejection by one's ἔθνος and delivery to the Romans would be shame enough; now his own people call for his shameful death.

With Pilate's verdict of Jesus' innocence, the trial should be over ("I find no crime in him," 19:5, 6). But a new charge is made, which constitutes a new *challenge* to Jesus' honor: "By our law he ought to die, for he made himself the Son of God" (19:7). The crowds consider this "claim" to be so serious a charge as to warrant the death sentence. And so a new trial ensues to deal with the new charge.

Let us view this new charge from the perspective of honor and shame. In antiquity people were constantly "making themselves" something, that is, claiming a new and higher status or role (Acts 5:36). Hence the public accusation that Jesus *makes himself* something functions as a *challenge* to a perceived empty claim, a common phenomenon in antiquity (κενόδοξος and ἀλαζών ; see Acts 8:9; 12:22–23; Josephus, *War* 2.55, 60; *Ant.* 17.272, 278). This sort of challenge to Jesus occurred regularly throughout the narrative (1) "... *making himself* equal to God" (5:18); (2) "Who do you *make yourself* to be?" (8:53); (3) "You, a mortal, *make yourself* God" (10:33); (4) "He *made himself* the Son of God" (19:7); (5) "every one who *makes him-*

self a king . . ." (19:12). In the course of this narrative, the author has consistently dealt with this charge by dividing the charge/challenge: (1) it is *denied* that Jesus "makes himself" anything, but (2) it is *defended* that he is such-and-such (Neyrey 1988:20–23). For example, Jesus claims in 5:19–29 that he is "equal to God." This is no empty claim, for he insists that God has granted him both creative and eschatological powers and the honor attached to them. The Father (1) *shows* him all that God is doing (5:20), (2) *has given* all judgment to the Son (5:22), (3) *has granted* the Son also to have life in himself (5:26), and (4) *has given* him authority to execute judgment (5:27; Neyrey, 1988:20–25). Thus, Jesus does *not* "make himself" anything, for that would be a vainglorious claim and thus false honor. But he truly is "equal to God," "King," and "Son of God," because these honors, roles, and statuses are ascribed to him by God (see the ascribed honor of being "made king" in 6:15).

It is not, moreover, accidental in the Gospel traditions that Jesus himself rarely claims to be prophet, king, son of God, etc. These tend to be ascribed to him either by God (13:31; 17:5, 24; see Mark 1:11; 9:7) or by others: (Son of God, 1:34, 49; Christ, 1:41; 10:24; King, 1:49; 6:15; 12:13; Savior, 4:42; and Prophet, 4:19; 6:14). Thus the tradition steadfastly maintains that Jesus is an honorable person in two respects: he does not seek honor by making vain claims to such-and-such a status, but he is regularly ascribed great honor by others. The reader, then, has been schooled how to interpret this new charge against Jesus, rejecting any sense of a vainglorious claim and affirming the truth of the honor ascribed to Jesus.

The new forensic charge requires a new *cognitio* by the judge (19:8–11). Pilate asks the appropriate question in terms of honor and shame: "Where are you from (πόθεν)?" (19:9). True honor is ascribed honor; and ascribed honor is a function of one's father and clan or one's place of origin (Malina and Neyrey 1991a:32–34, 39–40; 1991b:85–87). Concerning place of origin, honor was earlier denied Jesus because he is from Nazareth, from which no good comes (1:46; see Titus 1:12). Paul claims honor by coming from Tarsus, "no mean city" (Acts 21:39), and Jerusalemites claim honor from being born there (Ps 87:5–6). Concerning father and clan, it is almost a universal phenomenon in the Bible that when characters are introduced or described, they are always identified as the "son of so-and-so" or the "daughter of so-and-so." For an individual's honor is bound with that of his or her father. The rules in the *progymnasmata* for writing an encomium all stress that writers begin their praise of someone by noting that person's family and place of origin (Lee: 188–206). All of the extant texts of the *progymnasmata* on writing an encomium start with praise for εὐγένεια, which consists in noting (1) origin (γένος), (2) race (ἔθνος), (3) country (πατρίς), (4) ancestors (πρόγονοι), and (5) parents (πατέρες). Hence Pilate tests Jesus with the appropriate question, πόθεν εἶ σύ, which may refer either to his "place of origin" (8:23) or his parents (6:41–42). But the question directly touches Jesus' honor.

Jesus now remains silent (19:9). He neither defends himself nor offers a riposte to the challenge. Silence in the face of accusation is very difficult to assess; but in an honor and shame context it would probably be read as a shameful thing (see Neh 6:8). To fail to give a riposte to a challenge is to accept defeat and so loss of honor.

Yet readers have already been socialized in just this aspect of Jesus' honor, and so the riposte has been given in advance. Knowledge of whence Jesus comes (πόθεν) and whither he goes (ποῦ) has been a major issue throughout the narrative. Outsiders either do not know (3:8; 8:14; 9:29) or falsely think they know (6:41–42; 7:27–28). Many times Jesus proclaims the correct answer, namely, that he descends from heaven (6:38), or that he descends from heaven and ascends back there (3:13; 6:62). Insiders like the blind man accurately deduce the true "whence" of Jesus because of his power to heal (9:30). And finally the reader is told that Jesus comes from God and returns to heaven (13:1–2). Thus readers can answer Pilate's question; they know "whence he is," namely, a person whose parent is none other than God and whose "country of origin" is no less than heaven. His honor, then, is secure in their eyes.

The narrative suggests that Jesus' silence *challenges* Pilate's power, for he responds with new questions: "Will you not speak to me? Do you not know that I have power to release you and I have power to crucify you?" (19:10). "Power" (ἐξουσία) is at stake; and power is an expression of honor. Although Jesus gives no riposte to this new challenge concerning his origin, he does in turn offer a counter-challenge to Pilate's claim of power: "You would have no power over me unless it were given you from above" (19:11). Hence Pilate's power is a relative thing. The truly powerful figure is not Caesar, from whom Pilate enjoys ascribed honor, but none other than God, from whom all power flows (John 10:29). Emperors, kings, and governors all owe their power and honor to God (Rom 13:1; 1 Tim 2:2; 1 Pet 2:13–17). This narrative, moreover, asserts that it is God's will and purpose that Jesus undergo this trial (John 12:27). God commanded that he "lay down his life and take it up again" (10:17–18). Inasmuch as sons are commanded "Honor your father" (Exod 20:12; Deut 5:16; Mark 10:19), the presentation of Jesus as the obedient one (Heb 5:8; see Mark 14:36//Matt 26:39//Luke 22:42) marks his actions here as honoring his Father and thus warranting the honor of an obedient son.

In fact, Jesus ironically states that even Pilate is behaving honorably because he acts in accord with the power given him from above. The dishonorable people are those "who have delivered me over to you" (19:11);

they are the sinners. Thus in the confrontation between him and Pilate, Jesus remains successful; he suffers no loss of honor. In fact, he seems to have gained an ally of sorts in Pilate, his judge, "who sought to release him" (19:12).

Final Verdict and Sentence (19:12–16). In the next scene, the grand public tableau of the trial, the two sets of contestants play another episode of challenge and riposte. In terms of the Pilate-vs-Jesus contest, Pilate's move "to release him" functions as a definitive riposte to the crowds' various challenges to Jesus' claims to honor. Pilate thrice declares Jesus innocent, and so Jesus cannot be shown to be "making himself" anything. But in terms of the Pilate-vs-crowd contest, the latter issues one final challenge, not so much to Jesus' claims, but to the honor and status of Pilate himself. "If you release this man, you are not Caesar's friend; anyone who makes himself a king sets himself against Caesar" (19:12b).

As historians remind us, a "friend" is often described as the object of political patronage (Bammel: 205–210; Brunt: 1–20). Thus Josephus, when speaking of a circle of aristocrats, calls them "persons of power among the Friends of the King" (*Ant.* 12.298); Antiochus wrote to his "governors and Friends" (*Ant.* 12. 134). Philo records how Flaccus acted harshly against those who "insult a king, a Friend of Caesar's, a person who had received Pretorian honours from the Roman Senate" (*Flac.* 40; cf. 1 Macc 2:18; 3:38; 10:65). Thus Pilate owes Caesar a debt of loyalty for his ascribed honor as procurator. Whatever honorable status he enjoys depends on his being the faithful client of an imperial patron. But Pilate's status as "Caesar's *friend*" (and client) is directly challenged by the crowds, who accuse him of shaming Caesar by supporting a rival king. Pilate answers this challenge in a scene in which all of the various challenges and ripostes are resolved.

Pilate's riposte takes the form of a solemn judicial verdict and sentence. But the scene as narrated contains a fundamental ambiguity. The text states that "he (Pilate) brought Jesus out and sat down at the judgment seat" (19:13). Controversy surrounds the verb "sat down" (ἐκάθισεν), which may be read transitively (i.e., Pilate *sat* Jesus *down* on the judgment seat) or intransitively (i.e., Pilate himself *sat down* on the seat). Grammatical studies support both readings. Those who argue that Jesus was seated point to the irony of the powerless Jesus assuming the role of judge, a role ascribed to him by God according to John 5:22, 27; and 12:31. This reading would follow the gospel axiom that last is first, weakest is greatest, the judged one is the judge. Indeed it would be an extraordinary piece of irony for the dishonored Jesus to assume this position of great honor (see Luke 24:26).

But the literal reading of the passage portrays Pilate's riposte to the crowd's challenge to him. As judge and magistrate in charge of these affairs, including the exercise of the *jus gladii*, Pilate now assumes all of the trappings of his office. Honor is replicated in bodily posture as Pilate seats himself on his official seat, the βῆμα, while the other participants stand (19:13). Exercising his authority, he issues a proclamation to the crowds: "Behold your king!" Rhetorically, this remark is a command ("Behold!") and an insult ("your king," see 18:39). It ostensibly upholds the original claims of Jesus by dismissing the challenges of the crowd. Thus the judge has rendered a third verdict of innocence (18:38; 19:4, 12), which functions as a riposte to the challenges to Jesus' honor. But the claim that Jesus is a king is no more acceptable to the crowds now than it was earlier.

Finally the two strands of the honor contests coincide. The crowds challenge Pilate's verdict, even as they shame Jesus: "Away with him... crucify him" (19:15a). Pilate had previously noted the shame of being disowned by one's own ἔθνος (18:35), which shameful action is now repeated. Ostensibly, Pilate has lost the game, and his honor has been diminished. But he makes one last move, a final riposte to the power of the crowd.

Inasmuch as "king" has been the contested claim throughout the trial, Pilate demands of the crowd a formal judgment in the case: "Shall I crucify your 'king'?" (19:15b). Questions, of course, are challenging, and the response to this question brings maximum shame on Jesus' antagonists: "We have no king but Caesar" (19:15c). Their remark is an act of supreme dishonor to their heavenly Patron and Sovereign. At the conclusion of the Greater Hallel we find the following prayer:

> From everlasting to everlasting thou art God;
> Beside thee we have no king, redeemer, or savior;
> No liberator, deliverer, provider;
> None who takes pity in every time of distress or trouble.
> We have no king but thee. (Meeks 1967:77)

It is they who prove to be the "friend of Caesar," thus shaming God and God's anointed king. Rensberger notes that Pilate has once more humiliated his opponents by having them publicly deny their claims to a political messiah (96). Yet no reader would fail to note that God is now mocked and must vindicate his divine honor. The advantage seems to lie with the crowd who bends Pilate to its will and succeeds in dishonoring Jesus ("Crucify him!" 19:15).

A judicial sentence is pronounced, but one which is fraught with irony. The official judge, Pilate, apparently yields in this game of push and shove; his sentence is hardly honorable or just. Jesus' accusers, who earlier claimed that they had no legitimate authority to put a man to death (18:31), finally succeed in a plot that began in 5:18 and was solemnized at a rump trial in 11:50–53. Their success in having Jesus killed would be a mark of honor for them in the eyes of observers, but readers of the narrative know that this "sentence" is fully within the control of Jesus (12:32–33; 10:17–18) and the will of God. The sentence of a shameful death, then, is but an apparent loss of honor.

4. *Title (19:19–22).* The game of push and shove continues over the public title attached to Jesus' cross. Pilate's inscription, "Jesus of Nazareth, King of the Jews," may be read as a final ironic riposte by the narrator in defense of Jesus' honor, comparable to Caiaphas's "prophecy" about Jesus' death (11:51). It is also Pilate's act of authority in defense of his own embattled status. The title, which may be construed as another honor claim, is once again challenged by the Jerusalem elite, who urge a more shameful version: "'This man said, I am King of the Jews.'" Again, they charge that Jesus vaingloriously assumes honors not rightfully his (19:7, 12). This time Pilate wins: "What I have written, I have written" (19:22).

5. *Crucifixion (19:17–37).* The normal sequence of events which accompanies crucifixion was listed at the beginning of this study. In view of that, the shameful elements narrated in the crucifixion of Jesus in the Fourth Gospel are the crucifixion itself, with Jesus' position as the middle figure in a triptych of criminals, themselves shameful persons (19:18). The mocking title over the cross publicly challenges Jesus' claim to honor and status. He is apparently stripped naked, for his clothing is confiscated by his executioners (19:23–24). The synoptics all record various persons "mocking" him (Mark 15:27–32; Matt 27:38–43; Luke 23:35–36), which is absent from the Fourth Gospel's account. Yet the very scene is a public humiliation (John 19:20); spectators would give public witness to the shame of Jesus' death (see Philo, *Spec. Leg.* 3.160). Thus to them he dies a brutal death, apparently a victim whose life was taken from him in violent fashion. His blood is spilled, without hope of vengeance or satisfaction. This is what outsiders see and count as shameful.

The narrator, however, instructs insiders to perceive this scene in terms of honor. First, Jesus does the honorable thing by his mother. She is presumably a widow, and now her only son is dying. In that culture, she has no male (husband or son) to defend her; she will suffer a tragic loss of honor with this death. But Jesus defends her honor by adopting as "brother" the Beloved Disciple, and by ensuring that his new kinsman will defend his mother's honor by "taking her into his own house" (19:27; see Acts 1:14).

Shame lies both in being a victim and more especially in the exercise of power by another over one's life. That may be what the eye sees in Jesus' death, but not what the ear hears in the narrative. Jesus is honorably presented as the figure in control of events. He *knows* that all is now completed (v. 28) and he *chooses* to die, "It is finished" (v. 30). Because the narrative has prepared us for this scene, we are not reading these honorable ideas into the text. Back in the exposition of the role of the Noble Shepherd in John 10, Jesus explicitly described the honorable character of his death. First, he knows it, and so manifests control over his life: "I lay down my life" (10:17); "I lay it down of my own accord" (10:18). Second, he is no victim; no one shames him by taking his life: "No one takes it from me" (10:18); no one shames him by having power over him: "I have power to lay it down and I have power to take it again" (10:18b). Just as he manifested control and power at his arrest, so he is presented here as doing the same thing. Honor is thus maintained.

Finally, his body was mutilated, a shameful act (recall the treatment of Hector's body by Achilles; see 1 Sam 31:9–10; 2 Sam 4:12; Jos. *Ant.* 20.99). The soldiers intended to break his legs and thus hasten death. Yet Jesus is spared this humiliation because he had already died. Moreover, the text puts an honorable interpretation on this by comparing Jesus' body to the paschal lamb, none of whose bones were broken (Exod 12:46; John 19:36). He dies, then, "unblemished." Nevertheless his chest is pierced, the wanton mutilation of a corpse. Yet as Josephine Ford has shown, the piercing of Jesus' side yields both blood and water, which in rabbinic lore constitutes a kosher object (1969:337–38). And so the narrator rescues Jesus' honor by indicating that this mutilation was controlled by God's prophecy through Zech 12:10.

6. *Jesus' Burial (19:38–42)*. Under other circumstances, the bodies of the crucified might be left to rot on the cross and become food for scavengers (see Rev 19:17–18). This final shame precluded reverential burial by kin, both a mark of honor and a religious duty. Yet in our narrative, purity concerns demand some rapid disposal of the corpses; and so the body of Jesus is buried.

This gospel narrates that Jesus' body received quite an honorable burial, despite the shame of his death. Joseph and Nicodemus bring a prodigious quantity of spices, "a mixture of myrrh and aloes, about a hundred pounds," enough spices for a royal burial (see 2 Chron 16:14 and Jos. *Ant.* 17.199). They perform the honorable burial ritual, "binding the body in linen cloths with the spices, as is the burial custom of the Jews" (19:40). A new tomb is at hand, wherein they honorably lay Jesus. Despite the shame of crucifixion, some honor is maintained by this burial.

V. Summary And Conclusions

As we learn more about the pivotal values of honor and shame in their cultural setting, we come to appreciate how the narrative of Jesus' passion is perceived and articulated in this perspective. Honor and shame are not foreign categories imposed by an alien culture, but values rooted in the very cultural world of Jesus and his disciples, whether Roman, Greek, or Judean. We have observed what these ancient people value, how they strive either to gain or maintain their reputation, and how honor is replicated in the presentation and treatment of the physical body. When we appreciate the typical form of a challenge/riposte encounter, we gain greater clarity into the common social dynamics of the male world of the first century in all its agonistic flavor. It is always tempting for modern readers to psychologize biblical characters, often imposing on them modern notions of the self or motivations and strategies typical of the modern world. Appreciation of the ancient psychology of honor and shame offers more authentic cultural and historical reading of those social dynamics.

Our understanding, moreover, of the cultural dynamics of honor and shame is a necessary and welcome addition to the standard tools of historical criticism. Our use of them greatly aids in the fundamental task of interpreting documents from a culture quite different from our own. And our appreciation of these cultural phenomena can only aid in our sympathetic understanding of other biblical and ancient documents, which share the same cultural values.

As a result of this study, readers of biblical documents should be able to apply the understanding of honor and shame to other texts. Using honor and shame as a template, readers can then bring to light the social dynamics operative, for example, in most of the public scenes of Jesus and his opponents. Whenever Jesus appears in public, the scene is generally described as a challenge to his claims of honor. The same perspective can profitably be applied to the conflicts between Paul and his opponents. Always honor is at stake, either as claimed or challenged. Thus no study of conflict in the biblical texts would be complete without its assessment in terms of the cultural dynamics of honor and shame. The bibliography contains further perspectives on honor and shame in relation to other biblical documents.

Works Consulted

Adkins, Arthur W. H.
    1960   *Merit and Responsibility: A Study in Greek Values.* Oxford: Oxford University Press.

Alföldi, Andreas
    1970   *Die monarchische Repräsentation im römischen Kaiserreiche.* Darmstadt: Wissenschaftliche Buchgesellschaft.

Bammel, Ernst
    1952   "*Philos tou Kaisaros.*" *TZ* 77:205–10.

Benoit, Pierre
    1952   "Prétoire, Lithostroton et Gabbatha." *RB* 59:513–50.

Blank, Josef
    1959   "Die Verhandlung vor Pilatus: Jo 18:28–19:16 im Lichte johanneischer Theologie." *BZ* 3:60–81.

Brown, Raymond E.
    1970   *The Gospel According to John XIII-XXI.* AnB 29A. Garden City, NY: Doubleday and Company.

Brunt, P.A.
    1965   "'Amicitia' in the Late Roman Republic." *Proceedings of the Cambridge Philological Society* 191:1–20.

Culpepper, R. Alan
    1988   "The Death of Jesus: An Exegesis of John 19:28–37." *Faith and Mission* 5:64–70.

Daube, David
    1973   *The New Testament and Rabbinic Judaism.* New York: Arno.

de Jonge, Marinus
    1977   *Jesus, Stranger from Heaven and Son of God.* SBLSBS 11. Missoula: Scholars.

Derrett, J. Duncan M.
    1989   "Christ, King and Witness (Jn. 18, 37)." *Bibliotheca Orientalis* 31:189–98.
    1990   "Peter's Sword and Biblical Methodology." *Bibliotheca Orientalis* 32:180–92.

Dodd, Charles H.
    1963   *Historical Tradition in the Fourth Gospel.* Cambridge: Cambridge University Press.

Douglas, Mary T.
    1966   *Purity and Danger. An Analysis of the Concepts of Pollution and Taboo.* London: Routledge and Kegan Paul.

Duke, Paul D.
    1985   *Irony in the Fourth Gospel.* Atlanta: John Knox.

Ehrman, Bart D.
    1983   "Jesus' Trial before Pilate: John 18:28 - 19:16." *BTB* 13:124–31.

Flusser, David
    1984   "What Was the Original Meaning of *Ecce Homo*?" *Immanuel* 19:30–40.

Ford, Josephine M.
    1969   "'Mingled Blood' from the Side of Christ (John xix.34)." *NTS* 15:337–38.

| 1991 | "Crucifixion, Epitome of Shame or Honour in the Ancient World?" Unpublished paper delivered in March 1991 to the Context Group, Portland, OR. Forthcoming in *Redemption as Friendship*. |
| 1992 | "'Let Her Take Up Her Cross and Follow Me.' The 'Crucifixion' of Women in Antiquity." Unpublished paper delivered to the Mid-West SBL convention in 1991. Forthcoming in *Redemption as Friendship*. |

Foster, George
    1967   "The Image of Limited Good." Pp. 300–323 in *Peasant Society: A Reader*. Ed. J. Potter, M. Diaz, and G. Foster. Boston: Little, Brown, and Company.

Friedrich, Paul
    1977   "Sanity and the Myth of Honor: The Problem of Achilles." *Journal of Psychological Anthropology* 5:281–305.

Garnsey, Peter
    1970   *Social Status and Legal Privilege in the Roman Empire*. Oxford: Clarendon.

Giblin, Charles H.
    1984   "Confrontations in John 18,1–27." *Bib* 65:219–32.
    1986   "John's Narration of the Hearing before Pilate (John 18,28–19,16a)." *Bib* 67: 221–39.

Gilmore, David, ed.
    1987   *Honor and Shame and the Unity of the Mediterranean*. Special Publication of the American Anthropological Association 22. Washington, D.C.: American Anthropological Association.

Haas, N.
    1970   "Anthropological Observations on the Skeletal Remains from the Giv 'at ha-Mivtar." *IEJ* 20:38–59.

Hengel, Martin
    1977   *Crucifixion*. London: SCM

Hewitt, Joseph W.
    1932   "The Use of Nails in Crucifixion." *HTR* 25:29–45.

Hill, David
    1987   "'My kingdom is not of this world' (John 18.36). Conflict and Christian Existence in the World According to the Fourth Gospel." *IBS* 9:54–62.

Lee, Thomas
    1986   *Studies in the Form of Sirach 44–50*. SBLDS 75. Atlanta: Scholars.

Malina, Bruce J.
    1981   *New Testament World. Insights from Cultural Anthropology*. Atlanta: John Knox.

Malina, Bruce J. and Jerome H. Neyrey
    1988   *Calling Jesus Names. The Social Value of Labels in Matthew*. Sonoma, CA: Polebridge.

1991a "Honor and Shame in Luke-Acts: Pivotal Values of the Mediterranean World." Pp. 25–66 in *The Social World of Luke-Acts: Models for Interpretation*. Ed. Jerome H. Neyrey. Peabody, MA: Hendrickson.

1991b "First-Century Personality: Dyadic, Not Individualistic." Pp. 67–96 in *The Social World of Luke-Acts. Models for Interpretation*. Ed. Jerome H. Neyrey. Peabody, MA: Hendrickson.

Meeks, Wayne A.
1967 *The Prophet-King: Moses Traditions and the Johannine Christology*. NovTSup 14. Leiden: E.J. Brill.
1972 "The Man from Heaven in Johannine Sectarianism." *JBL* 91:44–72.

Moxnes, Halvor
1988a "Honour and Righteousness in Romans." *JSNT* 32:61–77.
1988b "Honor, Shame and the Outside World in Paul's Letter to the Romans." Pp. 207–18 in *The Social World of Formative Christianity and Judaism*. Ed. Jacob Neusner. Philadelphia: Fortress.

Nagy, Gregory
1979 *The Best of the Achaeans*. Baltimore: The Johns Hopkins University Press.

Neyrey, Jerome H.
1987 "Jesus the Judge: Forensic Process in John 8:21–59." *Bib* 68:509–42.
1988 *An Ideology of Revolt. John's Christology in Social-Science Perspective*. Philadelphia: Fortress.
1993 "Clothing" and "Nudity." Pp. 20–25 and 119–125 in *Biblical Social Values and Their Meaning: A Handbook*. Ed. Bruce J. Malina and John J. Pilch. Peabody, MA: Hendrickson Publishers.

Nicholson, Godfrey C.
1983 *Death as Departure. The Johannine Descent-Ascent Schema*. SBLDS 63; Chico, CA: Scholars.

Pfitzner, Victor C.
1976 "The Coronation of the King: Passion Narrative and Passion Theology in the Gospel of St. John." *LTJ* 10:1–12.

de la Potterie, Ignace
1982 "La mort du Christ d'apres Jean." *Studia Missionalia* 31:19–36.
1984 "Le symbolisme du sang et de l'eau en Jean 19, 34." *Didaskalia* 14:201–30.
1989 *The Hour of Jesus. The Passion and Resurrection of Jesus According to John*. New York: Alba House.

Reinhold, Meyer
1970 *History of Purple as a Status Symbol in Antiquity*. Bruxelles: Latomus.

Rensburger, David
1988 *Johannine Faith and Liberating Community*. Philadelphia: Westminster.

Schnackenburg, Rudolf
1982 *The Gospel According to St. John*. New York: Crossroad.

Schneider, Johannes
1968 "Timê." *TDNT* 8.169–80.

Senior, Donald
    1991   *The Passion of Jesus in the Gospel of John*. Collegeville, MN: Liturgical.

Sherwin-White, A.N.
    1963   *Roman Society and Roman Law in the New Testament*. Oxford: Clarendon.
    1965   "The Trial of Christ." Pp. 97–116 in *Historicity and Chronology in the New Testament*. Theological Collections 6. London: SPCK.

Steinberg, Leo
    1983   *The Sexuality of Jesus in Renaissance Art and in Modern Oblivion*. New York: Pantheon/October.

Sylva, Dennis D.
    1988   "Nicodemus and His Spices (Jn. 19.39)." *NTS* 34:148–51.

Weber, Hans-Ruedi
    1979   *The Cross: Tradition and Interpretation*. Grand Rapids: W. B. Eerdmans.

THE ANTHROPOLOGY OF HONOR AND SHAME: CULTURE, VALUES, AND PRACTICE

John K. Chance

INTRODUCTION

The study of value systems has had a rather checkered career in anthropology. The 1950s and 1960s witnessed a few attempts to deal with values comparatively, such as the volume edited by Kluckhohn and Strodtbeck on various groups in New Mexico and Oscar Lewis's controversial portrayal of the values of the urban poor in capitalist societies. But by and large, anthropology has tended to merge values, as desired standards for behavior, with its concept of culture (as Lewis did with his model of the "culture of poverty"), and deny them any privileged status. After all, anthropology was—and some would say still is—supposed to be holistic, and to dwell on values at the expense of other aspects of cultural systems was deemed to be rather narrow. More to the point, though, is the fact that until very recently, cultural anthropologists have never dealt very well with the affective dimensions of culture. We have reveled in "structures" and "systems" of all kinds, from the Radcliffe-Brownian to the Levi-Straussian; and we have used all manner of power-laden idealist concepts such as "ideology," "hegemony," and the like. Yet the realm of the emotions, which are indisputably connected to values, has been banished to a small corner of psychological anthropology and has not received comparable attention.

Seen in this light, the anthropology of the Mediterranean is something of an exception. All ethnographic areas develop their own literatures, favorite themes, pet theories, and to a great extent, even styles of analysis. In the Mediterranean, analyses of the values of honor and shame have held a pivotal position beginning with the pioneering work of Campbell, Peristiany, Pitt-Rivers, and others in the 1950s and 1960s. "Honor and shame" is one of those topics on which any Mediterranean ethnographer can be expected to have an informed opinion, regardless of whether or not it has figured in his or her own research.

As one who is familiar with Mediterranean culture but does research in another part of the world, I am struck (once again) by the parochial quality of much anthropological writing. Area specialists tend to latch on to certain salient cultural features and promote and discuss them tirelessly among themselves. All too rarely are their insights read and considered by specialists in other regions, even when significant cultural affinities are known to exist. To mention just one example: as a Latin Americanist who works in Mexico, the comparative value of the Mediterranean honor and shame literature is obvious to me. Yet references to it in Latin Americanist ethnography are exceedingly rare, even in works on *machismo* and gender roles.[1] Thus for better or for worse, the values of honor and shame have emerged as hallmarks of Mediterranean cultures, despite their importance in some other parts of the world as well.

ANTHROPOLOGICAL APPROACHES

The papers in this volume might give the unwary reader the impression that anthropologists are largely in agreement on the meaning and significance of honor and shame in Mediterranean contexts. This is most definitely not the case, however. Just as the concepts themselves differ in meaning and nuance from one place to another, anthropologists have sought to explicate them in various ways. Cultural, psychological, symbolic, ecological, economic, political, and social structural interpretations have been offered, and a consensus on the fundamentals has been no easier to reach than it has been on anything else that anthropologists study. For instance, while many would agree that honor and shame are rooted in attitudes toward sexuality, Brandes, for one, has expressed doubts. Davis (98) has argued that sexual behavior is secondary, and that honor is essentially a system of social stratification that "describes the distribution of wealth in a social idiom."

The thorny problem of origins also remains unresolved. Schneider (18) has suggested that women first became a repository for family or lineage honor in the Mediterranean in pastoral societies that controlled limited and unpredictable resources. Under such conditions, the reasoning goes, the values of honor and shame and a preference for marriage within the group give the family or lineage a corporate identity and a patrimony to be protected. Women become a scarce resource and a correspondingly high value is placed on their virginity. Schlegel (727–29) has recently challenged this view, however, arguing that property relations and the practice of the dowry, rather than pastoralism *per se*, are fundamental. Disbursing property through the dowry, as is commonly done in the Mediterranean, makes it desirable for parents to guard their daugh-

---

[1] The concept of "shame" has also played an important role in studies of Japanese culture, but there it means something different. See Asano-Tamanoi for a comparative treatment.

ters' virginity. In societies where wealth, rank, or other forms of stratification differentiate categories of people, family status may be crucial to marriage arrangements. Female virginity thus serves to discourage male social climbing through seduction by ensuring that undesirable suitors cannot claim marriageable women by making them pregnant.

Still other aspects of honor and shame will likely be debated for some time. One frequently voiced criticism is that researchers often unthinkingly adopt the male point of view and fail to acknowledge that women may see things differently (Abu-Lughod 1986, 1990; Dubisch; Lever; Wikan). Lever in particular has argued that since the existence of a shared value system is problematic in any stratified society, anthropologists' preoccupation with honor and shame may obscure the lack of acceptance of these values by subordinate groups, especially those of gender and class.

Then there is the problem of how far to generalize findings from a single local community. This has always been a conundrum in anthropology, and it seems to have reached crisis proportions in Mediterranean studies. Researchers who become overly enamored of their concepts run the risk of distorting their data, and most ethnographers are uneasy about the prospect of lumping all parts of the Mediterranean together in one large honor and shame complex. Herzfeld has been the most vocal about this danger. He points out that while there does seem to be a substratum of connections among moral, ecological, and kinship variables in Mediterranean societies, the facts of variation and considerable differences in local terminologies must be taken seriously. He warns that "Massive generalizations of 'honour' and 'shame' have become counterproductive" (Herzfeld: 349).

Contributions of Biblical Scholars

Against all this theoretical and methodological ferment—most of it a product of the last 15 years—the Bible as a text for analysis presents some formidable difficulties. Most of these are well known: the authorship of particular books and passages is usually unknown and often multiple; dates are impossible to assign because of frequent revisions and distillations over the years; and the male point of view predominates throughout (with the notable exception of the Song of Songs; see below). In addition, those who seek to apply anthropology to the Bible face the problem of what ethnohistorians call "upstreaming:" how to validly project insights gained in the twentieth century—usually through ethnography—back into the distant past. Once eagerly embraced as a method for integrating ethnography and history (Fenton 1952, 1966), upstreaming's dubious assumption that the cultures that anthropologists study are characterized more by continuity than by change has been increasingly called into question.

Today's anthropologists are less naive than they used to be about the supposed autonomy of "traditional" societies, and they have become more sophisticated in their use of history.[2] While I do not espouse the extreme position that ethnography cannot be used at all for historical inference—after all, where would archaeology be today without ethnographic analogy?—I do emphasize that we must tread very carefully here. Of the papers in this volume, those by Neyrey and Hanson take the greatest pains to document the historical validity of Mediterranean honor and shame by noting the work of other scholars. This is important: enthusiasm for ethnography must not be allowed to result in the neglect of historical evidence, vague and incomplete as it often is on questions of values.

In contrast to the diverse approaches to honor and shame in the anthropological literature, the biblical scholars in the present volume all seem to draw from the same well. The implicit touchstone seems to be the 1966 volume *Honour and Shame*, edited by J.G. Peristiany, and particularly the classic essay it contains by Julian Pitt-Rivers on "Honour and Social Status," which together laid the foundation for most subsequent work on the subject. The present papers by Neyrey and Hanson give the clearest depiction of the biblical scholars' basic model, which has the following characteristics:

> (1) Honor and shame form a value system rooted in gender distinctions in Mediterranean culture. Preservation of male honor requires a vigorous defense of the shame (modesty, virginity, seclusion) of women of the family or lineage.
>
> (2) Honor, most closely associated with males, refers to one's claimed social status and also to public recognition of it. Shame, most closely linked with females, refers to sensitivity towards one's reputation, or in the negative sense to the loss of honor.
>
> (3) Mediterranean societies are agonistic, or competitive. Challenges to one's status claims (honor) are frequent and must be met with the appropriate ripostes. The ensuing public verdict determines the outcome, and whether honor is won or lost.

I found it refreshing to read the work of scholars who seek to use anthropology constructively. The positive tone and implicit adherence to a common analytical model have their benefits, and stand in sharp contrast to the disagreement, self-doubt, and bickering which characterize so

---

[2] The argument that traditions regarded as old are often more recent "inventions" has been very influential in recent years, and carries with it an implicit critique of the assumptions behind upstreaming (see especially Hobsbawm and Ranger; O'Brian and Roseberry). Sometimes the invention is done by anthropologists themselves; for an example from Mesoamerica see Chance and Taylor.

much current anthropological writing. If the biblical scholars show little inclination to get involved in the theoretical issues surrounding honor and shame (as most anthropologists who write on the topic feel they must), they may be excused on the grounds of discipline and training. On the other hand, as so often happens when one discipline borrows from another, the anthropology employed in these papers is beginning to look a bit dated. In what follows I will compare and evaluate the papers in terms of three basic themes: male versus female, local versus international, and values versus practice. These issues hardly exhaust the topic of honor and shame; they are simply the most salient ones raised by the authors in this volume.

Male versus Female

While all the authors seem to agree on the centrality of gender distinctions in Mediterranean patterns of honor and shame, only two of them touch significantly on the female half of the equation. Stansell provides a sensitive analysis of family relationships in the David narratives, particularly the shame surrounding the rape of Tamar. As a micro-sociological account of events and relationships, this piece succeeds quite well. Yet the reader gets little feel for the larger picture. What were the general contours of the society and culture in which these events took place? Even more to the point, how were the family and the lineage structured in ancient Israelite society? Kin relationships cannot be understood fully unless they are situated in these cultural contexts. While Stansell addresses these matters in occasional comments and in the conclusion of the paper, a fuller discussion would be welcome. Granted, it would have to be somewhat speculative, but I see that as an unavoidable part of the enterprise.

The only paper that deals explicitly with the female point of view is Bergant's analysis of the Song of Songs. This is one of the few biblical passages to give women a direct voice, and thus has special significance for the topic at hand. Not surprisingly, these poems celebrating the joys of physical love do not readily lend themselves to honor and shame analysis. Here we find a female protagonist voicing the sort of thoughts and sentiments to which a modest woman of shame would be loathe to admit—at least in public. Bergant's analysis is even-handed, and she is careful not to push the honor and shame model into areas where it doesn't apply. At the same time, I find her essay unnecessarily inconclusive. The question should be asked: Why does this poetry deviate from the expectations of the model? One possible answer is to construe the poems as a protest against—or an assertion of disaffection with—a system of gender relations that severely restricts the expression of female sexuality. A parallel can be drawn between the female voice in the Song of Songs and the contemporary Bedouin women's oral poetry studied recently by Abu-Lughod (1986). Both express highly emotional sentiments that differ radically from those found in ordinary everyday language and behavior, where the discourse of honor is more likely to predominate. The poems suggest defiance of the public moral system (of honor and shame), yet Abu-Lughod found that they do not jeopardize the reputations of those who recite them.

> This discourse seems to be opposed to the mundane discourse of ordinary language structured by overt social values and honor-linked personal ideals. Individuals whose ordinary actions and statements conform to the modesty code, who take pains to present themselves as moral and worthy of respect, use poetry to comment on their personal fortunes and tribulations in love and to express sentiments that violate the canons of modesty. Poems are vehicles for the expression of attachments to sweethearts or spouses that, if communicated in everyday social interaction, would damage reputations and jeopardize claims to respectability and, at the individual level, would ordinarily undermine self-image and self-presentation. (Abu-Lughod 1986:232)

If we follow Abu-Lughod's lead and look at it in this way, the Song of Songs invites us to reflect on the relationship between the public morality of honor and shame on the one hand, and the private sentiments of subordinate groups (such as women) on the other. In particular, the Song of Songs could be taken as evidence to support the feminist critique of honor and shame discourse as a male-centered value system that does not accurately represent the beliefs of women. While I find this interpretation attractive, it admittedly makes the question of how the Song of Songs came to be canonized more puzzling than ever.

Local versus International

While ethnographic studies of honor and shame have been resolutely local, focusing on individuals and families in small communities, several writers have noted in passing that the model can also be applied to larger social wholes, even entire nations. Simkins attempts just this in his analysis of the Book of Joel. The people of Judah, he suggests, suffered shame in the eyes of other "nations" because they abandoned the cult of Yahweh in the face of a catastrophic plague of locusts. This may be a plausible interpretation, but I do not find it a compelling one. Shame, of course, depends on public opinion, and in order to fulfill its potential, the model ought to specify the values and opinions held by the community of reference. This is, of course, most difficult to do at the "international" level and constitutes the weak link in Simkins' argument. In this case the other "nations" are defined only by what they are not: those outside the community of Yahweh. This being the case, one could ask why they should be especially concerned if the people of Judah abandon a cult which the people of these other nations do not share? Conversely, why should the Judeans feel especially shamed in the eyes of other peoples who hold different religious beliefs? Why should the Judeans find Joel's admonitions compelling? The honor and shame argument, if it is to answer these questions convincingly, should spell out in more detail the values that all these nations have in common, despite their religious diversity.

Difficulties of this sort underscore why the best studies of honor and shame have come from local settings. I find Davis's (78) remarks persuasive:

> Honour is local; it cannot be measured or assessed, except very roughly, by an outside observer. Nor can unattached outsiders be assessed readily, for that implies a moral relationship.

Biblical texts present different kinds of challenges in this regard. The David narratives which Stansell analyzes are rich in detail on family relationships, but have less to say about the values and attitudes of the wider community. Here the interpreter must struggle to avoid an analysis that is "too local"—too close to particular individuals and insufficiently cognizant of the community culture (which furnishes the all-important "public opinion") in which they live. The Book of Joel poses the opposite problem, though in the end it demands a similar solution. Here we confront the big picture on an "international" scale, and the challenge is to avoid an interpretation that is not local enough. In both instances, though, the task of the analyst is similar: to supply an appropriate profile of the local society and culture of the actors. This is, to be sure, rarely an easy thing to do when working with historical texts. Ethnographies must be utilized creatively toward this end, but only, I would caution, in conjunction with other historical materials which lend them credibility and allow the researcher to avoid the pitfalls of excessive upstreaming.

Values versus Practice

Social analysis often distinguishes between normative statements of value on the one hand, and actual behavior or practice on the other. Put another way, beliefs about how things "ought to be" in the view of the anthropologist's informants are distinguished from how things "really happen" as measured by the anthropologist's own observations of behavior. A good deal of theoretical ink has been spilled by opposing camps of ethnographers who would privilege one approach over the other, and this is not the place to rehearse those debates. I raise the issue only to make two general points. First, written texts composed for didactic or inspirational purposes, such as those of the Bible, generally tend to emphasize the normative point of view (though details of actual events may not be totally lacking). Second, the relationship between peoples' values, particularly public ones like honor and shame, and those same peoples' ongoing social relationships is never isomorphic and is in fact highly problematic.

While the second point applies to some degree to all human societies, some ethnographers have found the problem to be especially acute in Mediterranean culture, where in Gilmore's (180) words, "Everywhere there is a contradiction of 'appearance and reality.'" Avowals of social egalitarianism coexist with marked socioeconomic stratification; an ideology of male dominance often contrasts with a reality of matrifocality and a reliance on affines rather than agnates; the high value placed on family solidarity and the loyalty of siblings is counterbalanced by frequent intra-family hostilities; agonistic perceptions of one's neighbors coexist with strong sociocentric sentiments; and women are said to be inactive economically despite their important contributions to the domestic economy (Gilmore 180). These are just some examples; the list could grow much longer. Gilmore (180) refers to these contradictions collectively as a condition of "structural dualism." Feminists have made similar observations, noting "the ways in which cultural ideologies regarding gender roles may misrepresent or obscure the actual power Mediterranean women wield in daily life" (Dubisch 272).

It is important to keep this "structural dualism" in mind when studying written texts such as the Bible, which may provide only fragmentary information. The Bible has obvious advantages for the study of values, which as cultural concepts can best be approached in texts through close attention to language. For this reason I find the papers by Hanson and Stansell, both quite sensitive to Hebrew and Greek terminology and problems of translation, to be the most persuasive analyses. By contrast, Neyrey's paper on the Johannine passion narrative takes a different tack. Here the text itself contains fewer value terms, and the analysis is more behavioral than linguistic. Claims, challenges, and ripostes as forms of behavior are all evaluated in terms of the honor and shame model. While I do not dispute Neyrey's interpretation, I find it less than totally convincing because evidence of the meaning of the various episodes to the actors themselves is in such short supply. Are they acting on values of honor and shame which they hold, or is the author (and the reader) perhaps unwittingly projecting his analytical model onto the data?

Another problem in Neyrey's analysis is the generality of the model employed to analyze challenges and ripostes in dramatic episodes in which Jesus is seized and charged with crimes. Such dramatic events serve as a reminder that all stratified societies hold values that to some degree are analogous to "honor and shame." Indeed, vivid portrayals of how these work in the United States in the highly charged context of crime and punishment appear nightly on our television screens. The problem posed by the passion narrative is how best to elucidate that which is peculiarly *local* or *Mediterranean* on the basis of largely behavioral data.

The relationship between values and practice is also at issue in Bergant's paper on the Song of Songs. I would argue that the values expressed in these poems do not necessarily translate into overt behavioral characteristics (independent sources of information would be necessary to establish that). Thus, the appropriate question here is not whether the Song of Songs represents the practice of a particular group or social class, but whether or not it signifies distinctive values held by members of that group or class. In this case, the *values* are at odds with Mediterranean notions of female shame, yet it is quite possible that the *actions* of the people represented in the poems were quite conventional. We may never know for sure.

As important as it is, however, recognizing the gap between values and practice does not take us nearly far enough. The honor and shame literature amply documents "structural dualism," but there has been little attempt at explanation. Such a task, I suggest, requires an adequate theory of culture. An older cultural anthropology assumed that the societies it selected for study were culturally homogeneous. The investigator's job was to describe the rules, patterns, or recipes that people followed, though it was unclear just why they should follow the rules or even how many of them did. Attempts to deal with these problems have led to the current accent on cultural heterogeneity, exercise of power and domination (even in so-called "egalitarian societies"), and further probing of the relationship between culture and practice. In this view, culture does not consist of rules to be followed blindly, but is rather "a structure of conflicting premises within which the struggle for dominance [takes] place" (Peristiany and Pitt-Rivers: 4). A concept of culture that accommodates conflict and dominance surely brings us a step closer to understanding "structural dualism," but as Abu-Lughod (1986:171) reminds us, we also need to examine how an ideological or moral system "can be understood to shape what individuals do and say, and perhaps even feel . . . ." This is the central question of what has come to be known as "practice theory."

Abu-Lughod (1986, 1990) addresses this problem as she tries to clarify the relationship between Bedouin women's poetry of romantic love and the more austere (at least for women) public values of honor and shame. Though expressed through traditional forms, the poetry carries sentiments that violate the public code and may be seen as a form of resistance to it. Yet this resistance comes from within, not from outside the system of power, and it is possible to speak of "two ideologies in Bedouin culture, each providing models of and for different types of experiences" (Abu-Lughod 1986:258). Because she clarifies aspects of both culture and practice, and because she shows the limits of the values of honor and shame by describing areas of experience where they do not apply, Abu-Lughod's work offers promising leads for future research.[3]

Conclusion

I have argued that biblical scholars who seek to apply anthropological concepts would do well to (1) recognize the possibilities for heterogeneity in the societies they study, (2) develop a more sophisticated concept of culture, and (3) pay more attention to the relationship between values and practice. To conclude, I will briefly mention three other challenges of a more methodological nature that I think ought to be considered.

The first has already been mentioned: Herzfeld's admonition that blanket applications of a monolithic model of honor and shame should be avoided. I agree that the ethnographic corpus has now reached the point where Herzfeld's critique must be taken seriously. But where does this leave the field of biblical criticism? The authors in this volume have not heeded Herzfeld's call: they have employed a common model and applied it to peoples diverse in time and space. Yet they can hardly be blamed for doing so, since the historical—not to mention the biblical—literature lags far behind the ethnographic where Mediterranean values are concerned, and has not yet reached the required critical mass that would enable a more comparative style of analysis. That time will surely come, and this volume itself will hasten its arrival. But at present, biblical studies of Mediterranean values seem to be at a stage similar to that which characterized anthropology at the time of publication of Peristiany's seminal *Honour and Shame* (1966). Like those in that volume, the papers here show that a research tradition is emerging; once perfected, it will stimulate new work which will be in a better position to engage in a more nuanced, comparative form of analysis.

My second point may seem obvious, but it is worth mentioning: there is more to Mediterranean culture than honor and shame. The Bible can be fruitfully approached with other insights from anthropology, and their enthusiasm for gender-based values should not cause biblical scholars to lose sight of other possibilities. Dubisch (272), for example, notes that the honor and shame literature, preoccupied as it is with issues of sexuality

---

[3] Another innovative attempt to explicate the relationship between culture and practice is Ortner.

and dominance, has failed to consider the significance of gender "in a wider, more complex social and cultural web." She uses field data from Greece to show that gender concepts may be used to establish and maintain the boundaries between different social groups. Her approach downplays differential power between males and females and emphasizes instead the spatial and social separation of the sexes. This is not the place to go into the details of her argument; I would simply note that even the oft-studied topic of sexuality has significant cultural aspects which have received little attention from researchers interested in Mediterranean values.[4] This point is just as applicable to historical and biblical studies as it is to ethnographic ones.

Finally, there is the matter of history. There is ample evidence apart from the Old and New Testaments that questions of honor (and probably shame) loomed large for ancient Greeks, Romans, and Judeans (see, for example, the historical works cited by Neyrey and Hanson in this volume). Yet anything which might be called a *history* of honor and shame remains an elusive goal. The papers in this volume provide valuable time depth, but the analyses—like most others in the literature—are remarkably static. We still have little understanding of how various conceptions of honor and shame changed over time in accord with alterations in their social and cultural contexts.[5] This is hardly surprising, since the genre itself was launched by ethnographers, few of whom are equipped or inclined to *do* history. Historians of the Mediterranean, on the other hand, are preoccupied with other topics most of the time, and it would be unrealistic to ask them to shoulder all the burdens of a cultural history of the region. This is why interdisciplinary scholarship of the sort presented here is so important. Now that ethnographers are addressing spatial variations in Mediterranean values, biblical scholars with an anthropological bent are well-positioned to begin to explore comparatively their vicissitudes through time.

---

4 See Delaney for a recent ethnography of a Turkish village which considerably illuminates this topic.

5 One major anthropological exception to this generalization is Caro Baroja's masterful historical analysis of honor and shame in Spain.

WORKS CONSULTED

Abu-Lughod, Lila
1986 *Veiled Sentiments: Honor and Poetry in a Bedouin Society*. Berkeley: University of California Press.
1990 "The Romance of Resistance: Tracing Transformations of Power Through Bedouin Women." *American Ethnologist* 17:41–55.

Asano-Tamanoi, Mariko
1987 "Shame, Family, and State in Catalonia and Japan." Pp. 104–120 in *Honor and Shame and the Unity of the Mediterranean*. Ed. David D. Gilmore. Washington, D.C.: American Anthropological Association Special Publication No. 22.

Brandes, Stanley
1987 "Reflections on Honor and Shame in the Mediterranean." Pp. 121–34 in *Honor and Shame and the Unity of the Mediterranean*. Ed. David D. Gilmore. Washington, D.C.: American Anthropological Association Special Publication No. 22.

Campbell, John K.
1964 *Honour, Family, and Patronage*. Oxford: Oxford University Press.

Caro Baroja, Julio
1966 "Honour and Shame: A Historical Account of Several Conflicts." Pp. 79–138 in *Honour and Shame: The Values of Mediterranean Society*. Ed. J.G. Peristiany. Chicago: University of Chicago Press.

Chance, John K. and William B. Taylor
1985 "Cofradias and Cargos: An Historical Perspective on the Mesoamerican Civil-Religious Hierarchy." *American Ethnologist* 12:1–26.

Davis, J.
1977 *People of the Mediterranean: An Essay in Comparative Social Anthropology*. London: Routledge and Kegan Paul.

Delaney, Carol
1991 *The Seed and the Soil: Gender and Cosmology in Turkish Village Society*. Berkeley: University of California Press.

Dubisch, Jill
1993 "'Foreign Chickens' and Other Outsiders: Gender and Community in Greece." *American Ethnologist* 20:272–87.

Fenton, William N.
1952 "The Training of Historical Ethnologists in America." *American Anthropologist* 54:328–39.
1966 "Field Work, Museum Studies, and Ethnohistorical Research." *Ethnohistory* 13:71–85.

Gilmore, David D.
1982 "Anthropology of the Mediterranean Area." *Annual Review of Anthropology* 11:175–205.

Herzfeld, Michael
    1980   "Honour and Shame: Problems in the Comparative Analysis of Moral Systems." *Man* 15:339–51.

Hobsbawm, Eric and Terence Ranger, eds.
    1983   *The Invention of Tradition*. New York: Cambridge University Press.

Kluckhohn, Florence Rockwood and Fred L. Strodtbeck, eds.
    1961   *Variations in Value Orientations*. Evanston, IL: Row, Peterson & Co.

Lever, Alison
    1986   "Honour as a Red Herring." *Cultural Anthropology* 1:83–106.

Lewis, Oscar
    1965   *La Vida: A Puerto Rican Family in the Culture of Poverty—San Juan and New York*. New York: Random House.

O'Brien, Jay and William Roseberry, eds.
    1991   *Golden Ages, Dark Ages: Imagining the Past in Anthropology and History*. Berkeley: University of California Press.

Ortner, Sherry B.
    1989   *High Religion: A Cultural and Political History of Sherpa Buddhism*. Princeton: Princeton University Press.

Peristiany, J.G.
    1966   "Honour and Shame in a Cypriot Highland Village." Pp. 171–190 in *Honour and Shame: The Values of Mediterranean Society*. Ed. J.G. Peristiany. Chicago: University of Chicago Press.

Peristiany, J.G., ed.
    1966   *Honour and Shame: The Values of Mediterranean Society*. Chicago: University of Chicago Press.

Peristiany, J.G. and Julian Pitt-Rivers
    1992   "Introduction." Pp. 1–18 in *Honor and Grace in Anthropology*. Eds. J.G. Peristiany and Julian Pitt-Rivers. New York: Cambridge University Press.

Pitt-Rivers, Julian
    1961   *The People of the Sierra*. Chicago: University of Chicago Press.
    1966   "Honour and Social Status." Pp. 19–78 in *Honour and Shame: The Values of Mediterranean Society*. Ed. J.G. Peristiany. Chicago: University of Chicago Press.

Schlegel, Alice
    1991   "Status, Property, and the Value on Virginity." *American Ethnologist* 18:719–34.

Schneider, Jane
    1971   "Of Vigilance and Virgins." *Ethnology* 9:1–24.

Wikan, Unni
    1984   "Shame and Honour: A Contestable Pair." *Man* 19:635–52.

AN ANTHROPOLOGIST'S RESPONSE TO THE USE OF SOCIAL SCIENCE MODELS IN BIBLICAL STUDIES

Gideon M. Kressel
University of Beer-sheva

Each of the studies in this volume will be examined separately in this response. The critiques are intended to provide a note of caution as well as to be helpful in future study of honor and shame in the biblical materials.

Bergant, D. "The Song of Songs"

The Song of Songs is, indeed, exceptional within the current Middle Eastern (not necessarily all Mediterranean) cultures. A specific focus of Bergant's study is the relationship between women and men, relative to the issues of honor and shame. However, Bergant does not demonstrate an awareness of the distinction between the mores regarding sex in interpersonal relationships and those regarding sex as a symbolic extension of the hierarchical relationship of agnatic groups. Desire in the Song speaks of mutual fulfillment (the woman is not being used, she is actively loving), and is a celebration of love as seen, principally, from the woman's viewpoint. The passion of the Shulammite is never indecent and nothing is demure about it.

There is no sign that it impinges on the honor of her group of agnates, an entity that had existed in Israelite society, but not in the same way it does among the Arabs. The association of male power with status that constitutes gender-based categories of honor and shame are not applicable to the Song. The canonical status of the Song shows that it revealed an authentic facet of life, another normative facet of a people (the biblical Hebrews) that couldn't be concealed. The Bible (mostly Deuteronomy) has much to say about adultery, but little is said about virginity and sex prior to wedlock. Although the man is instructed to marry the virgin he has raped (Exod 22:16), this is not a matter of life and death, but, rather, of the amount of the brideprice (Patai). The most likely reason for this is that such an event would not have impinged upon conventional scales of social esteem vis-a-vis the lineages of the groom and the bride (see Kressel: Chs 2–5). The alluring power of the woman's eyes concurs with the perception of female seductiveness. In the Song, the man is as captivating to the woman as she is to him, which seems to mean that the practice of matchmaking was not the special concern of the young couples' parents.

In the Middle East the role that the brothers and paternal cousins have assumed with regard to women corresponds to an agnatic setup, where group cohesion is a primary concern and males are the guardians of female sexuality. The woman in the Song spurns the supervision of her agnates, so the implication for the agnate group of the woman's lovemaking is not, in the Bible, as extreme as found throughout the Middle East today. There is no underlying concern for the agnatic groups power and status and, consequently, there is no interest in controlling what might threaten it. The sexual activity of the woman is neither suppressed nor supervised. It is no wonder that the 'Song of Songs', which recounts mutual love between women and men, has been omitted from those parts of biblical texts that are brought to public awareness for Muslims. The Song of Songs, therefore, remains vertually unknown throughout the Middle East.

Simkins, R.A. "Joel and the Theme of Shame and Honor "

Joel's call for his people to return to God is contingent on the honor/shame idea, although, within a very distinctive understanding, which is the idea of the chosen people in the Old Testament. An initial question is, why did God chose one single people? An answer can be seen (Scharf-Kluger) in the inner dynamics of the total election event: it had to be some people, for God's sake. That it was Israel may be related to Israel's difficult situation, which prepared it to follow an inner way (as opposed to the "outer way," which depends on the use of force to obtain goals). They were a poor peasant people, living on the edge of the Fertile Crescent and the desert, exposed to ecological misfortunes (such as droughts), eternally oppressed by the surrounding great kingdoms, Egypt and Babylon. They could make room for themselves only inwardly, and were therefore peculiarly suited to take upon themselves the misery and dignity, the curse and blessing, of God's election. They were, so to speak, God's easiest prey.[1] This may be suggested in the motif of the "lowly origin" of the bearer of salvation, as in Deut 7:6ff, where the smallness of the people is pointed out. The election comes into full light as a consciousness-creating phenomenon, for had man not accepted it, the world would have dissolved back into its original unconscious state.

---

[1] Being one of a number of peoples, such as the Armenians and the Gypsies in modern times, who were subjected to persecutions and were the victims of genocide, the Jews can claim, throughout history, to have been the object of God's rage. Such patterns of persecution are often interpreted as divine punishment for disobedience. In a figurative sense, therefore, the people are God's prey.

According to Joel, a catastrophe that afflicts the Jewish people casts shame on it, since it evinces perfidy of its divine predestination. There is precisely the "four-fold" covenant model of sin-judgment-repentance-blessing. Return to God means here individuation of the moral commandments, to avert catastrophe.

All through the generations Jews are requested to repent, thereby protecting their future. Based on this pattern of thinking, a trend has developed among some Orthodox Jews which attributes the Holocaust to disregard of the commandments by the non-observant Jews. This is based on an endemic trait of Jewish society, not necessarily shared by other Mediterranean peoples. In sociological terms, it has been suggested (Durkheim) that society is to be equated with God. In that sense, the sacred represents the social being. Thus, all the commandments serve the purpose of reenforcing the maxim "You shall not do to your neighbor what is abhorrent unto you." It is precisely in this sense that individual comportment impinges upon the fate of the nation. Therefore Joel calls for repentance.

Simkins searches in vain for details as to what was wrong with the people's behavior (". . . for Joel to interpret the natural catastrophe as Yahweh's judgment on the people without at the same time ascribing to them guilt, or sin, is intolerable with respect to our understanding of God") One should bear in mind the Jews' awareness that they provide God's "easiest prey," and that the constant consciousness of guilt is a feeling to be overcome by ritual praying and doing good deeds for others.

The cruelty of fate indicates a punishment for disobeying the commitment to repent. Natural catastrophes or defeat in battle evince the absence of God, who is supposed to defend the people, and thereby brings on a sense of shame. This can be found in all religious wars that transcend the Middle East and the Mediterranean. The sense that "God is on our side" can be found in the history of Europe during the Crusaders' time and was a component of the 30 Years' War of Protestantism and Catholicism. This exists to this very day, vehemently, in the Muslim perception of a "holy war" and their battle cry that their God (Allah) is the greatest.

Stansell, G. "Honor and Shame in the David Narratives"

David's faults, as described in the Bible, are essentially different from the perception of impropriety that prevails in the Middle East, his being personal defects. Honor and shame in the Middle East pertains to the individual as well as the group. There is no mention as to which of David's wrongs slight his tribal group. Like many Bible protagonists, David is fallible, imperfect, and never saint-like. This is in contrast with Jesus "who never said a mumbling word" or Muhammad's *'ismah* (Sharon: 65, 80), that is, a person without any blemish whatsoever and completely infallible. The agnatically-steered perception of moral behavior in the Middle East would mean an alignment with one's group through war and peace.

The Bible examines the righteousness of even the most self-assured person in a way reminiscent of Jewish prayer during the High Holy Days:

> We have trespassed, we have been faithless, we have robbed, we have spoken basely, we have committed iniquity, we have wrought unrighteousness, we have been presumptuous, we have done violence, we have forged lies, we have counseled evil, we have spoken falsely, we have scoffed, we have revolted, we have blasphemed, we have been rebellious, we have acted perversely, we have transgressed, we have persecuted, we have been stiff-necked, we have done wickedly, we have corrupted ourselves, we have committed abomination, we have gone astray, and we have led astray.

We see here internalizing of a sense of guilt and shame. Therefore, psychology, rather than anthropology, found the biblical text grist for its mill.

The rituals pertaining to the investiture of a king did not yet have a solid tradition. David was only the second king in Israel's history. In other societies, the sanctification of power often requires the future sovereign to transgress the rules of the commoners (e.g., committing incest), to be surrounded by a wall of taboos, and he is also condemned to an unnatural death. A great many of the shameful acts the Bible cites with regard to David are those he committed in the capacity of a commoner, a sinful being, but these were transferred to his person also as king because there were no special norms of kingly behavior. The tension between the prophet Samuel's opinion (1 Sam 8:11–18) and that of the people expressed the needs of an earthly kingdom. The misunderstandings that evolved between Saul and Samuel did not stem from fault-finding in the usual sense (regarding commoners). It had to do with Samuel's understanding of what the Kingdom of God and the spirit of God implied. All these found expression in the interrelationships between King Saul and David. With the anointing of David by Samuel, the spirit of God, according to the Bible, is transferred to David, although Saul was still the king. This is what disrupted the relationship between Saul and David (Scharf-Kluger: Part 2).

The first dynasty in the world of Islam, the Ummayads, were removed by the 'Abbasid (in 750 CE) through a great massacre. Thus for the Abbasid dynasty, the confilict with the Ummayads was a tribal conflict that did not involve removing the spirit of God from the opposite side, as it did in the case of Saul and David. However, once the conflict was over and the Ummayads had been slain, the Abbasids took this as evidence that God must have been on their side, or, as it is often said: "[our] God is bigger [*Allahu Akbar*, i.e., bigger than their God]."

Hanson, K. C. "How Honorable! How Shameful!"

Hanson relates makarisms and reproaches, two (in fact one) types of biblical expression, to the "agonistic" nature of Mediterranean cultures. I find this idea stimulating for reasons that are implicit, but inadequately developed in the article. However, my reasons for endorsing this idea carry us beyond the confines of the Mediterranean, because social values that motivate *homo agonisticus*, i.e., the wish to be honored and to avoid the consequences of being ashamed, are omnipresent and are not the monopoly of the peoples of the Mediterranean (cf. Stewart). Hanson is germane, noting that the purpose of makarisms and reproaches is the effort to disrupt competition over righteousness. Thus the course of "Pharisaism" may set individuals into meriting honor by fulfillment of religious commandments. However, the confounding of righteousness' tracks seems to mark Jesus' style (Matt 5:3–10 and 23:13–36).Yet, dismissing haughtiness and advocating humility cannot be done through a "religion of rote"; i.e., religion cannot prescribe an alternative commandment. The "Sermon on the Mount" inculcates a "folkway" (in W.G. Sumner's use of this term), and helps the audience memorize the moral of the story. Replacement of vanity by meekness is susceptible to frustration. It is by and large abortive because haughtiness and humility are complementary and dialectically opposed, as is cogently explained by the Maggid of Zlotchov (d. 1786, see Buber: 144). They [the disciples] asked the Maggid of Zlotchov:

> All the commandments are written in the Torah. But humility, which is worth all the other virtues put together, is not stated in it as a commandment. All we read about it is the words in praise of Moses, saying that he was more humble than all other people. What is the significance of this silence concerning humility? The rabbi replied: "If anyone were humble in order to keep a commandment, he would never attain to true humility. To think humility is a commandment is the prompting of Satan. He bloats a man's heart telling him he is learned and righteous and devout, a master in all good works, and worthy to think himself better than the general run of people; but that this would be proud and impious since it is a commandment that he must be humble and put himself on a par with others. And a man who interprets this as a commandment and does it, only feeds his pride the more in doing so.

Another anthropological feature of the biblical language observed by Hanson in reference to the use of makarisms, on the one hand, and admonitions, on the other, is the way in which both of these forms differ from blessing and cursing. Attentive to Hanson's critique of Janzen's handling of the text (1965:223–26), I find myself on the side of Janzen. As an anthropologist, I can bolster Janzen's arguments by providing three kinds of clarification.

1) While blessing and cursing entail the application of magic, beatitudes and reproaches do not. Blessing is meant to secure a better life with the help of God; cursing aims at harming the well-being and future chances of a person. While blessing and cursing concern the future, makarisms and admonitions pertain to the present. They clearly delineate an attitude (positive or negative) with regard to a pattern of present behavior, but do not aim to help or harm someone's well-being and future. Rather, makarisms and admonitions draw attention to remarkable people in the attempt to set up their behavior as exemplary, to be learned from and imitated by others.

2) Praiseworthy individuals whose personalities become a paragon and a living example of their society, are thereby in danger of being envied and harmed by the "evil eye". Hanson correctly draws attention to the implication of envy, but he errs in interpreting the casting of the evil eye as a malevolent (purposeful) activity. Couched in anthropological terminology (cf. Lessa and Vogt: 245ff), the evil power contained in witchcraft is put to work unintentionally, viz. often by looking, touching or merely being jealous, without evil intent.

Unlike sorcery, a category containing magic of all sorts, which is practiced, witchcraft is derived or radiates from within. Neither the manipulation of objects or the casting of spells is employed. Deified individuals, who are natural targets of envy are therefore encompassed with mana, a Polynesian term used by anthropologists to refer to a non-individualized supernatural force. The mana is believed to operate like an armor, protecting the holy person. Witchcraft, as well as magic and divination, are undoubtedly world-wide and lasting anthropological phenomena. Although their roots are in antiquity, they still exist in the modern world, where anthropologists can discern them despite changes in the form of revelation.

3) The connotations of honor and shame in the writing of Matthew do not encompass the case of any particular Mediterranean code of honor and shame. While Matthew is concerned with the channels one establishes with the omnipresent (which include harmony with other persons and with oneself), the code that is said to bespeak Mediterranean societies engages scales of honor (and shame) that determine society's internal hierarchy (Kressel). The orientations are as different as they can be from one another, and the heart of the matter is greater concern for cultural nuances. Reference to the Arab world, on the one hand, and to Mediterranean Europe, on the other, as if they are one cultural entity, has recently raised an objection (cf. Herzfeld 1980), if not a protest (Piña-Cabral) against the intellectual legacy that made this association possible.

Jerome Neyrey "Despising the Shame of the Cross"

The anthropological model of honor and shame, selected here as a template for reading John 18–19, is not appropriate for this assignment. John's Jesus has an immense personal honor, and not only in the eyes of the narrator but also, as he describes it, in the eyes of the Jewish priesthood. It is not dishonor that they feel toward him. On the contrary, they respect him and the impact of his words to the extent that they want to see him removed. Jesus posits a danger to their creed, social position, and worldview in general. John 18–19 relates the story of a counter-challenge to the challenge implemented by means of an executioner, rather than a scenario of a claim, challenge, and riposte. Jesus' dialogue with his executioners resembles in principle the brief exchange Archimedes had with his executioners 250 years earlier (212 BCE). While engaged in drawing a mathematical figure on the sand, and being uninterested in the preponderant political event of that moment (occupation of Syracuse by the Romans), Archimedes asked an intruder to step aside (in order to avoid casting his shadow over the drawing). The soldier's response was to run his sword through Archimedes' body. No blame attaches to the Roman general, Marcellus, since he had given orders to his men to spare the house and person of the sage. The story graphically demonstrates, however, that a man may be too absorbed in his own work to appreciate that even a simple request, "Please do not disturb me!," can result in fatal consequences.

I do not find that the sentences exchanged between Jesus and his (Jewish) adversaries, and between Jesus, his adversaries, and the Roman, Pilate, run along the principles of mockery or derision contests, such as those which are reported in the anthropological literature (see e.g., Balikci). The events leading to the crucifixion of Jesus hinge on problems pertaining to the legitimation of his teachings and on sovereignty, inter and intra the Jewish people. Problems such as these are to an extent endemic and particular to the Jewish society. To some extent they are ubiquitous and lasting; i.e., they cannot be taken as a reflection of ancient Mediterranean culture, pertaining to honor and shame.

Moreover, the Gospel according to John regards Jesus' spiritual merits as they are revealed to his disciples, persecutors, and the divine. The text concerns the dimension of Jesus' persona, and the religious implications of the conflict between him and his people. These are important constituents of the historical eventualities, but do not necessarily explain nor are they explained by cultural traits pertaining to honor and shame in either the Middle East or in the wider Mediterranean culture area during the time of Jesus or the present.

Cutting himself off from the ethics of the Pharisees, announcing that his kingdom is not of this world, Jesus places honor on a multi-level metaphor; they advocate achieving vindication in a way that can be seen by others, and he advocates achieving righteousness beyond material and social interests. One might question to what extent Jesus is honest; whether he was aiming at achieving divinity in the eyes of his followers as opposed to raising the social level of ethical rectitude.

CONCLUSION

The accent in the studies on honor and shame in this issue of *Semeia* oscillates between the concomitants of agnation (patrilineally tribal) and the vindication of what the individual person does in the eyes of God (viz, not necessarily in terms of what others expect him to do). On the Southern (Muslim) littoral of the Mediterranean basin, the agnatic ethics (i.e., the etiquette of the tribe, the extension of which is the *ummah*) is the essence of the spiritual, in contrast with the material interests of households. On the European (Christian) littoral, the individual accountability vis-a-vis the divine is the moral code, which conflicts with individual material interests. Honor operates differently; you can be dishonorable in the eyes of your fellowmen and yet honorable in the eyes of God. The two littorals once encountered are at cross-purposes and the absurd can come into play.

The word *religion* expresses a subjective relationship to certain metaphysical, extramundane factors. The meaning and purpose of religion lie in the relationship of the individual to the divine, or the path of salvation and liberation (as in Buddhism). To be the adherent of a creed which gives expression to definite collective belief, is not always a religious matter but more often a social one and, as such, it does nothing to give the individual any foundation (Cf. Jung 1953:157).

Works Consulted

Balikci, Asen
    1970   *The Netsilik Eskimo.* Illinois: Doubleday & Waveland. Buber, Martin
    1947   *Tales of the Hasidim; Early Masters.* New York: Schocken Books.

Buber, Martin
    1947   *Tales of the Hasidim: Early Masters.* New York: Schocken Books.

Durkheim, E.
    1968   *The Elementary Forms of Religious Life.* London: Allen & Unwin [1912, 1915].

Herzfeld, Michael
    1980   "Honor and Shame: Some Problems in the Comparative Analysis of Moral Systems." *Man* 15:339–351.

Jung, Carl G.
    1953   *The Collected works of C.G. Jung.* Vol. 12 Princeton: Princeton University Press.

Kressel, Gideon M.
    1992   *Descent Through Males.* Wiesbaden: Otto Harrassowitz.

Lessa, William A. and Z. Vogt Evon
    1958   *Reader in Comparative Religion.* New York: Row, Peterson and Company.

Patai, Raphael
    1959   *Sex and Family in the Bible and the Middle East.* New York: Doubleday.

Piña-Cabrel, Joãode
    1989   "The Mediterranean as a Category of Regional Comparison: A Critical View." *Current Anthropology* 30:399–406.

Schärf-Kluger, Rivkah
    1974   *Psyche and the Bible.* Zürich: Spring Publications.

Sharon, Moshe
    1989   *Judaism, Christianity and Islam: Interaction and Conflicts.* Jerusalem: Sacks.

Stewart, Frank H.
    1994   *Honor.* Chicago: The University of Chicago Press.

Sumner, William Graham
    1979   *Folkways and Mores.* New York: Schocken Books [1910].

SOCIETY OF BIBLICAL LITERATURE

Jameson and Jeroboam
Roland Boer

This book is the first major application of the work of Fredric Jameson to the Bible. Jameson, one of the leading literary and cultural critics working today, has developed a complex Marxist model of interpretation which includes a full range of issues from text to economics. The book has two sections, the first of which is a critical account of Jameson's approach. The second part applies that approach to the texts of the Jeroboam narrative in the Hebrew Bible (1 Kings 11-14; 3 Reigns 11-14; and 2 Chronicles 10-13). The examination of these texts moves from questions of form and content, through ideology and religion, to class and economics.

"...a major contribution both within and beyond biblical studies."—*David Jobling*

Code: 06 06 30 390 pages
Cloth: $44.95 ISBN: 0-7885-0116-X
Paper: $29.95 ISBN: 0-7885-0117-8

"What is John?"
Readers and Readings of the Fourth Gospel
Fernando F. Segovia, editor

This collection offers a fascinating and incisive look at the enormous diversity of approaches to and interpretations of the Gospel of John in contemporary Johannine studies in the United States. Both literary and theological approaches to the Gospel are included. In addition, a second group of essays assesses the state of Johannine studies at the close of the twentieth century. The essays of this collection were derived from presentations given in the Johannine Literature Section of the Society of Biblical Literature (1991-1993) and the 1994 Symposium "The Gospel of John at the Close of the Twentieth Century."

Code: 06 07 03
Cloth: $49.95 ISBN: 0-7885-0239-5
Paper: $29.95 ISBN: 0-7885-0240-9

Despising Shame
Honor Discourse and Community Maintenance in the Epistle to the Hebrews
David Arthur deSilva

This work demonstrates how the author of the Epistle to the Hebrews radically transforms the meaning of terms such as "honor" and "loyalty" for the members of the Christian minority community he addressed. Thus, for example, "honor," a value that formerly supported kinship and political structures within the dominant Greco-Roman culture is transformed into a term that signifies support for the fictive kinship within, and commitment to, the values of the alternative, Christian culture. DeSilva's painstaking examination of how shame, honor, and benefaction helped to maintain the integrity of the Christian minority community will be of interest to students of rhetoric, interpreters of Hebrews, and persons interested in first century social relationships.

Code: 06 21 52 384 pages
Cloth: $39.95 ISBN: 0-7885-0200-X
Paper: $24.95 ISBN: 0-7885-0201-8

Scholars Press
P.O. Box 6996, Alpharetta, GA 30239-6996
Phone: 800-437-6692; Fax: 770-442-9742

SBL members receive a 33% discount on direct orders.

Liberating Insights

NONVIOLENT STORY
Narrative Conflict Resolution in the Gospel of Mark
ROBERT R. BECK
Foreword by Ched Myers. Proposes a new way of reading the Gospel of Mark, one that points to a challenging message of nonviolent resistance as reflected in the story of Jesus' life and ministry. Marks gospel portrays Jesus as a protagonist who does not avoid conflict, but enters into it without himself resorting to violence.
210 pages, $16.00 paper

DIVINE REVOLUTION
Salvation & Liberation in Catholic Thought
DEAN BRACKLEY
Foreword by Jon Sobrino. A compelling exploration of the relation between transcendent "salvation" and temporal "liberation." Brackley surveys the social-historical meaning of salvation in church teaching; explores the thought of three giants of Catholic theology in the twentieth century: Jacques Maritain, Karl Rahner, and Gustavo Gutierrez; and argues that the Catholic tradition has great potential to articulate a hope which responds to the suffering of the poor in our time.
220 pages, $19.00 paper

APOCALYPSE
A People's Commentary on the Book of Revelation
PABLO RICHARD
Shows how the most powerful readings of the Book of Revelation are through the eyes of the oppressed, living out their faith in the context of the modern empire. Richard highlights the parallel between the poor and persecuted community reading the text today, and the original context in which it was written.
150 pages, $18.00 paper

THE GOSPEL OF MARK
A Mahayana Reading
JOHN P. KEENAN
Offers a radically new reading of this most intriguing of the Synoptic Gospels: through the lens of Mahayana-Buddhist philosophy. Keenan provides an overview of different interpretive techniques in Markan scholarship and argues for the validity of a Buddhist approach.
500 pages, $25.00 paper

INTRODUCTION TO THE OLD TESTAMENT
A Liberation Perspective
ANTHONY R. CERESKO, O.S.F.S.
"... a real and readable book written by a teacher who understands the needs of students... Ceresko provides those of us who teach that important first course in biblical studies with a book we have needed for a long time."
—*Biblical Archaeologist*
336 pages, $21.00 paper

At bookstores or direct
MC/VISA 1-800-258-5838

ORBIS BOOKS
Dept. SA6, Box 302
Maryknoll, NY 10545-0302

www.ingramcontent.com/pod-product-compliance
Lightning Source LLC
Chambersburg PA
CBHW032259150426
43195CB00008BA/506